D1351693

CA

5/11/14
PAGE
LOOSE
DF

2 1 JUL 2012

'Before The Wish I had been feeling in a rut and very hopeless – life was just happening around me and I was trying to keep up with it, not really living in the 'now', always stressed and trying desperately to control the present and dreaming of a more exciting future and just seeing a blank. But so much good has come from the course that I cannot really express half of it – in short, I now believe in myself, I believe life has huge things ahead for me and I believe that I truly can 'make it happen' by being positive and focusing that thought, with benefit not just for me but also for those in my life and the others who I am yet to meet.'

Katriona, interior designer, London

'I wanted to do The Wish because I had some career issues that I wanted to make decisions about, and because it had been highly recommended by two close friends. Within two weeks I got my dream job; all my questions were answered. It was like I had permission for the first time . . . It helped me to find a different type of role that was not the obvious role I had been pursuing, which was amazing, and really opened up my perspective on myself and my new role in life . . . I feel much different – it's given me a lot of confidence in just believing in myself and my worth, which is fantastic! Just knowing who you are and what you have to offer – The Wish worked for me.'

**Susan, an industrial designer who
works in Sydney and London**

'The Wish shook my world view and system for beliefs to their core. Angela presents in such a practical, down-to-earth way that everything can be put into action immediately. One cannot deny what's demonstrated before one's eyes . . . The Wish was the most profound experience of my life.'

Gerry, bank analyst, Zurich

'I don't think they're particularly little changes I've made since The Wish. I feel they're big. I've definitely grown as a person and learned a lot about myself as a person – and my purpose. It's really, really helped me that way. I thought I was drifting along. Now I find that there is a road and it's really helped me to be strong on that road.'

Dee, owner of a hair salon in Paris

'My greatest fear is probably lack of control, or loss of purpose. I've lost my way a bit. Having heard about The Wish I thought it a great opportunity to try and find out what my new role should be, rather than what I'd thought it should be – and then go on to find out my real purpose and true role . . . And so far I think it's working, I'm really enjoying it!'

Adrian, graphic designer, Bristol

'The Wish fitted in with my own personal philosophy of life, where your thoughts can create your reality.'

Robert, IT specialist, Birmingham

'The changes that I've felt have been fantastic – really positive. I really feel that I've got control of my life.'
Jenny, human resources manager, based in London

'I think all of us have a sense of our soul but we're not really tuned into it that much. The Wish gave me a chance to explore that level, and also to think about how to bring more purpose to my life . . . The Wish . . . helps all of us to have a sense of our place in the universe.'
Sean, finance director, Tokyo

'I had no idea what I wanted; The Wish gave me the confidence I needed at the job interview the next day, and I got the job! I'm absolutely ecstatic, over the moon – in one day it changed my life completely.'
Susie, actress, London

The
Wish

How to make your dreams come true

ANGELA DONOVAN

HODDER &
STOUGHTON

First published in Great Britain in 2011 by Hodder & Stoughton
An Hachette UK company

1

Copyright © Angela Donovan 2011

The right of Angela Donovan to be identified as the Author of the Work
has been asserted by her in accordance with the Copyright, Designs and
Patents Act 1988.

All rights reserved. No part of this publication may be reproduced, stored
in a retrieval system, or transmitted, in any form or by any means without
the prior written permission of the publisher, nor be otherwise circulated
in any form of binding or cover other than that in which it is published and
without a similar condition being imposed on the subsequent purchaser.

A CIP catalogue record for this title is available from the British Library.

Hardback ISBN 978 1 444 72768 5
eBook ISBN 978 1 444 72770 8

Printed and bound by Clays Ltd, St Ives plc

Hodder & Stoughton policy is to use papers that are natural, renewable
and recyclable products and made from wood grown in sustainable forests.
The logging and manufacturing processes are expected to conform to the
environmental regulations of the country of origin.

Hodder & Stoughton Ltd
338 Euston Road
London NW1 3BH

www.hodder.co.uk

It's time to make your wish come true

LONDON BOROUGH OF SUTTON LIBRARY SERVICE	
30119 026 303 25 7	
Askews & Holts	Jul-2011
158	

Contents

Acknowledgements

As thought holds the greatest power, so this book has come into being with its own life force to attract all seekers with a love of knowledge and whose quest is for their own betterment through their 'knowing'.

I would like to express my indebtedness to the spiritual teachers of the past and to the late Rolf Alexander MD, whose pioneering work I found truly enlightening and which, along with other similar disciplines, greatly inspired my thinking before writing this book.

My deepest gratitude is to Maggie Hamilton of Inspired Living, whose own inner knowing was there way before the book was born, and to her enthusiastic

team at Allen & Unwin, all of whom have worked tire-
lessly to enhance the magic of the written words, thus
creating a dynamic process to initiate and transform
the lives of all those who take this journey. And then,
by no means least, there is the one who has always
been there for me – my agent Susan Mears, with her
unstinting motivation, friendship and support. I thank
you all.

I dedicate this book with love to the one who has
continually stood by me with courage and positive
support, in recognition of our dreams for the
greatest benefit of humanity on Planet Earth – my
husband, Andrew.

Introduction

There's been nothing quite like The Wish before. It seems miraculous to me that it has emerged now, at this point in time when so many of us have become fearful of what lies ahead and of what our future holds.

The sheer brilliance of The Wish is that it takes care of all that anxiety and shreds it, and in its place puts strength, hope, inspiration, restoring the magic of living and shifting us into a truly powerful, life-enhancing space.

It's also rewarding and life-affirming to know without a shadow of a doubt we can make it happen for ourselves. It is my belief that The Wish is the ultimate mind-medicine of the future. So I want everyone who seeks it – whether you're a student, CEO, small-business owner, shop assistant, parent or artist – to have the opportunity to benefit.

For over three years now I have been sharing The Wish with many people across the world and from all walks of life. And in many instances I have been made privy to the illuminating life changes people have gone through having done The Wish. These experiences have propelled me to write this book.

I know what you're thinking. At some time or other we've all had the urge to 'make a wish'. Each of us has done it countless times, and while some wishes do come true, we believe that most did so more through 'chance' or 'luck' than anything else. That view is nothing more than a simple mindset, and one you can quickly lose as you read on.

We've all had those moments in life when we feel just a tinge of disappointment with how our futures look – maybe you've finished a university degree and you're wondering 'what next?', your relationship or marriage has ended, you've lost your job or suffered a financial setback. Somehow the tables have turned and however much we try to lead brave new lives, the days, months, years ahead seem to be set in stone and we feel quietly despairing.

Yet, instead of getting lost in anxiety and regret, we are now going to begin to light up our lives with pure, inspirational thoughts, just like the ones we used to enjoy in our childhood. It's about clearing away the clutter and endless issues that block our true potential. As you'll soon see, there's no need for you to have any doubts or be in any way negative about 'making wishes'. This fresh approach has the potential to transform every aspect of your life – you can truly 'make it happen' for yourself with each wish you make. While at first you may feel you're on an uncharted journey, I promise it will be one you'll never forget. You will learn to map and manifest the very deepest secrets of true love, happiness, abundance and success in whatever form you wish them to take.

In the following chapters there are a number of easy exercises that can be done anywhere, at any time. They're simple, don't take long and, most importantly, they work. So, for example, while a lot of books talk about focusing your thoughts, few give you clear steps on how to do this. With The Wish I give you a golden key to open your mind to the immense power within you, yet this is only a small part of the magical process that will unfold as you read and absorb these pages. Soon you will have at your fingertips methods to help you be clear about who you are, where you're heading and a whole lot more. Through the insights I share, your life will become your very own creation, a plan of pure brilliance for living exactly as you want from this moment on. Health and wealth – in the richest sense of the words – and happiness are key components of these discoveries. When you can enjoy these life-enhancing qualities in your everyday life, you will naturally radiate a deep sense of love to those around you.

But the best is yet to come, as you experience for yourself how to make your heart–soul connection. Once you have this simple little technique under your belt, you're ready for the 'Soul Test', a fail-safe exercise which helps you link in with the wisdom of your soul. When you can enter into a dialogue with your soul, your life cannot help but be transformed. Imagine how you'll feel when people are touched by your presence – as they, too, become enlightened by that glow of joy within you!

So this is no ordinary 'wish' I'm talking about. You are about to realise your full potential to create and manifest by releasing your power through freedom of thought, giving you the self-knowledge to learn – at last – who you truly are and your reason for being here on earth at this time. You will discover how to command your thoughts and actions and ignite every aspect of your life more positively from now on – it is your divine right, and the passport to your own wonderful journey in and beyond this life.

With my love,
Angela

1

The wonder of wishes

The Wish is your gift to yourself. It's one of the most powerful gifts you will ever receive because it offers you the miracle of realising your deepest desires through the unique magical power you already hold within you. The Wish gives you the greatest opportunity to begin to transform your life, and much more.

Have you noticed how certain wishes come true, while others seemingly dissolve? You may wonder why this is, but don't worry – the how and why will be revealed as you read on. The key thing is that once you realise what you already hold in your hands, you'll be inspired to begin to dream again of all you wish for – for yourself, for those you love, for the world. Soon you'll discover how to stop losing your vitality. You'll learn how to energise yourself by tapping into the immense energy readily available to you. You'll also know which dreams will create a happier, more enriched life and which will turn things pear-shaped.

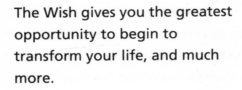

The Wish gives you the greatest opportunity to begin to transform your life, and much more.

While everyone wants their dreams to come true, sometimes life can seem quite overwhelming, leaving us feeling that it's just not practical or possible to achieve what we long for. Living day to day, taking care of ourselves and those we love, working and commuting, paying the rent or the mortgage can end up becoming the sum total of our lives. So we end up telling ourselves we haven't got the time, the energy or self-belief to do more than get by. Add to this the negative fallout from financial upheavals, climate

8

change, shaky governments, natural disasters, war and terrorism and we can so easily assume (or be led to believe) that we have to accept whatever comes our way.

No-one denies we live in challenging times and that not everyone has our best interests at heart. But when you understand how to make your wishes come true – and make no mistake, all you can create is well within your reach – life takes on a very different hue. Accepting that this is not just a possibility but achievable changes everything. You can really start to make wonderful things happen.

Whatever you've achieved up to now in your life, *that* is your journey, along with the setbacks, disappointments, blocks or frustrations along the way. You may have thought that nothing ever goes right for you. It's time to put all that negative stuff in a box, as it's in the past. Now it's time to look to the future with a lighter heart. Through The Wish you *will* feel empowered and you *will* be able to 'create' good things for yourself from this moment on.

As you'll see, even our darkest moments can offer

us wonderful ways forward. Often it's life nudging us to do things differently – to lighten up, get more sleep, take our health seriously, apply for a new job, take a holiday, make more time to spend with friends, get creative, move to a new suburb, invite more love into our lives. All these things are possible right now. There's no need to wait for some distant time in the future to make life how you would like it to be. No matter what you're facing right now, let me assure you it's time to go beyond the mundane stuff of everyday life so you can experience the beautiful completeness that is the real you.

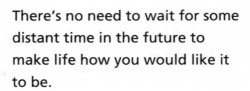

There's no need to wait for some distant time in the future to make life how you would like it to be.

The adventure you're about to take is a very practical and gentle one that will teach you real life skills, from how to heal past baggage and stop your energy being zapped, to connecting with your soul. This last point is crucial, because even though you may get everything you *think* you want, unless it resonates with the truth of who you really are, with your soul's needs, you'll never find happiness, success or fulfilment.

As we take The Wish journey, you'll see that dreams that come true aren't just chance occurrences. This flies in the face of popular opinion, but it's so. You may have noticed that anything you do that attracts good things always amazes others. They pass off your achievements as just being 'lucky'. Yet what we don't think about nearly enough is exactly what a 'lucky' person *is*. Some say people make their own luck, and to a great extent that's absolutely true, but the real question is: how can you capture this wonderful thing called 'luck'? The timeless knowledge I am now sharing with you will help create your own beneficial happenings, your own 'luck'.

The beauty of The Wish approach is that it delivers all this and more. As you read this book, you will see how the change in your approach to life will strengthen and empower you, and help set you on your chosen path – it will help you find out who you really are. The

The Wish

Wish will give you far greater awareness of how best to operate in the world, taking away all those nagging doubts and anxieties. When you're no longer on the roller-coaster ride of daily life, you'll be in the perfect space to discover what you truly want, to create the genuine joy and satisfaction you ache for. Why? Because you will be powerful beyond all imagining.

I was recently made redundant and wanted to change careers. And I was single and wanted a partner. Within two weeks I found I was talking to three different companies about international projects, and within days I met a man. To me The Wish is far more empowering than any other course I've done. I couldn't believe how quickly things changed.

– **Kathy, head of TV production, London**

2

The power of love

The supreme happiness in life is the conviction
that we are loved. *Victor Hugo*

As you might imagine, I have spent a long time
pondering the magic of 'wishing', checking it out and
testing it on many levels before I began to teach and
then write about it. As I thought about wishes I
realised that each was a tiny act of creation. More
than that, I discovered that all true creation is born
out of love. Why? Because love is all-encompassing,
it's that most exquisite quality that resides in the very
centre of who we are. When you stop to think about it,
you realise we cannot survive without love, and it's

through love that we live, flourish and willingly help others to do so. Through love we gain an overwhelming compassion for all living things.

All true creation is born out of love.

We will be examining love in greater detail shortly. Here, as we ponder its qualities, we begin to sense how love gives us the 'x-factor'. Love triggers our ability to make things happen because it dramatically increases our life energy. When we're in love, the world is a beautiful place, full of potential. Nothing gets us down, and we're hopeful about the future. Love is contagious; people *enjoy* being around us. They are inspired to be part of our dreams. And good things happen.

With love comes an enhanced power with which to focus our thoughts and everything we do. Through love we see how the alchemy of making wishes come true increases a hundredfold. You may have experienced this in lots of ways. One moment's inspiration to create a special birthday party for someone you love, and all the excitement that comes with it, can create a wonderful gathering that everyone enjoys. How does this work? Your love and positivity draw everyone to join in. Your excitement at making it happen becomes their excitement, so you can't help but create something special. This dynamic is as true for relationships as it is for a painter or sculptor, an engineer, a doctor, a mum. We're talking about life energy here, and love is one of the greatest aspects of the life force. Love does in truth 'make the world go round'. As we learn the intricacies of wish-making, we are also discovering the nuances of love – love for ourselves and each other.

Through love we see how the alchemy of making wishes come true increases a hundredfold.

Wish-making is also about discovering how to capture feelings – not just any old feelings, but the very highest

The Wish

level of feeling that we're capable of. So how does this work? Let me take you back to those wonderful dizzy moments when you were very young, when you had all the time in the world to dream, and believed all your wishes would come true. Recollect the thrill, the almost tangible sense of excitement you felt as each new wish welled up inside you. Remember how much joy you experienced as you took great delight in fashioning something so dear to your heart. Pause for a moment and recapture that feeling . . . How good is that? This is how you can feel right now if you so choose.

There's much more to this wonderful insight. When your childhood wish was fully formed there was a breathtaking sense of anticipation. Recall how each precious wish stayed with you, how it lingered. Back then you wanted your wishes to come true with every atom, every fibre of your being. You *felt* the energy of each wish you made. You knew it intimately. You also knew without a shadow of a doubt that this wish was taking place, that it would be just as you imagined. So then you let it go to the universe.

The power of love

These memories are golden moments. They can remind you of how wishes are formed and, regardless of what has happened since, I know these cherished moments are still there for you. These golden moments are still readily available to us when we give ourselves time to absorb and process their power.

So now I want you to allow yourself to feel that increasing inner glow again as you take yourself back to your childhood, to that time when the sun always seemed to shine, when the grass was always a cushion of emerald green and the sky the richest expanse of blue imaginable, to a time of shop windows bursting with Christmas toys, of exciting birthday parties, of trips to the zoo and the beach. Notice how exquisite it is to relive the pure joy of these experiences, and feel the utter sense of bliss they bring.

In many ways these moments feel like you are being let loose in your very own wonderland. There you are, free to create the very best and most beautiful of life's wishes and dreams, at a time when there are no limits on yourself. That was how it was for me. I used to lie there on the grass, eyes shut tight with an

17

innocent intensity of thought, avidly creating my dreams and willing them to come true.

Sometimes I would look up at the vast night sky with its endless array of stars – it all seemed so magical, and in fact it still does. The sheer scale of the cosmic force linking all creation was, and is, dazzling to behold. Being a person who never likes to waste a special moment, as a child I would have a big wish ready for the times when a shooting star whizzed past. I felt really lucky because there always seemed to be one passing when I needed one. Without thinking, I'd hold my breath as I made my wish and watch its golden thread streak by. Then I would hold the thrill and inner warmth of that magical experience close inside me.

The exquisite thing is that the magic of those moments still lives in me as I write this. Can't you feel this, too, as you read these words? Give yourself a moment to absorb the enormity of wishes; in a way, when we think about a time when a wish came true we are again experiencing that special moment when that wish was formed. Or to be more accurate, when

18

we make or recall a wish we're stepping beyond the here and now, as wishes are made outside of time.

This is one of the big insights we'll be working with. So, while you may well be thinking life has passed you by, the truth is that time does little to quell the immediacy of your dreams when they truly inspire you. With a little imagination you are still able to recapture the love and excitement you once experienced when you made a wish. But it's up to you to join the dots. As many a mother has said to her child, 'You can do anything if you only put your mind to it.' Or, put another way, everything is possible when you are ready.

3

What about me?

Have you noticed how you begin to feel hopeful again when you start to think about your dreams and wishes? That's because you suddenly shift to a different space. It sparks a sense of optimism, as if the impossible might just be possible. For too many people this is a new experience, as it's been a long time since they felt the least bit hopeful.

So why did we ever lose that genuine sense of vision that enables us to make our wishes come true? What went wrong? When did our belief in ourselves, in life's magic, stop? And why?

As we grow, the daily issues of life have a habit of getting in the way. Without realising, we often lose sight of the very things that make us feel happy and fulfilled, until we no longer believe wonderful things are possible for us, for those we love, for the planet. We settle for a 'lesser-than' existence, and our diminished way of life impacts on those around us as well, until we're all living in a space that inhibits our potential.

The sad thing is that while we're living in this lesser space, we don't recognise life's magic when it comes our way. We're too busy working to pay the rent or mortgage, to bring up the children, take care of the home. We just don't have any spare time for ourselves. At best we promise ourselves some 'me time' next week, next month or next year. Maybe we're so stressed and tired it's just all too much to think about now. Or perhaps we think we're not deserving of special things in life, or we've never realised that we can ask for things for ourselves.

I regularly hear such explanations and more when people come to see me. One thing they have in common is a tendency to put off what they truly wish for until at least tomorrow, and therefore never. So instead of seizing the moment and living for the sheer joy of life and what it can offer – which is how we're meant to live – we settle for whatever life throws at us and thus we never taste its magic. This way of seeing life creeps up on us. We don't just wake up one day and find ourselves in a bad space. It happens over weeks, months, often years.

We all need – and must have – our own 'me time'. While it isn't always easy to carve out time for ourselves, we must determine that somehow we will make it happen. So, how do we do this? To succeed we have to recognise and accept who we are and begin to truly value and love ourselves. So even if you're a stressed-out executive struggling with a heavy workload, or a hard-pressed student up to your eyes in exam papers, pause for a minute and give yourself an 'inspirational moment' to begin to create the very next thing you would like to take place in your life, right down to the way that you would like it to happen.

It's only when we have 'me time' that we get to know ourselves: it's an essential ingredient for success-ful wish-making. Just as importantly, we begin to build up a force of positive energy within and around ourselves. It gives us a firm foundation from which to start creating our lives as we want them to be. And believe it or not, by nurturing yourself and contemplating who you really are, you are already attracting 'luck', otherwise you wouldn't be reading these words right now. 'Me time' doesn't have to be complicated, but it does need to be fun, inspiring, nurturing. Take time out to enjoy a sensual bath or shower, then go and relax in comfy clothes while listening to your favourite music. 'Me time' isn't a luxury, because when you make yourself a priority, you quite naturally take yourself into a whole new space and time.

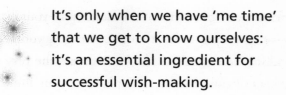

It's only when we have 'me time' that we get to know ourselves: it's an essential ingredient for successful wish-making.

When I met busy mum Carrie she told me she was feeling very tired, constantly battling with her teenage children and with no time or energy left for herself.

She sounded guilty about wanting 'me time'. However, by learning to make time every day for herself, Carrie stopped fretting over her difficult daughters, their infuriating, maddening mood swings and their constant expectation that she should do everything for them – and their subsequent lack of gratitude! Once she began to enjoy dedicated 'me time' each and every day, she saw how it reflected positively in her family and made everyone much less stressed.

If you're still in any doubt as to the importance of 'me time', I'd like you to imagine you are 97 years old and a journalist has come to interview you about your life. He asks you if there is anything you regret not doing. What would your response be? 'Ahh! There were *so* many things I could have done, but didn't do.' Please give this some thought. It's a question that shouldn't be dismissed lightly. This is *your* life, your moment of choice.

At the end of your life, will you regret that you were so busy working that you didn't recognise the value of the relationships and love that you had? Will you wonder what all that chasing after money was for when it had so little value in the end? Will you regret spending so much time at everyone's beck and call, never having time for the things you love? Will you wish you hadn't remained in the job you hated simply because it came with a dental plan and other perks? These are uncomfortable questions but they hold the key to freedom, so don't put them in the 'too hard' basket. This is exciting stuff!

Indeed, if you think about the way you would like your life to pan out you will get some powerful hints as to the way forward. This will help you begin to construct a better tomorrow. The great thing about 'me time' is that it helps you sort out what you *think* you need from what you *actually* need. Remember, there will never be a better time for you to start doing all those things you've always wanted or meant to do. So, please, no excuses. There's no need to procrastinate any longer. Do not finish your life in deep regret due to fear or ignorance.

It's time to see the big picture, and how much a part of the big picture you are. We are all spiritual beings who have existed beyond this, our present lifetime. We are all talented and courageous souls who have agreed to come here to learn and to grow, to be our fabulous best. And while there's a lot happening on the planet that can and does distress us, it's also a great opportunity. The decisions we make about our lives impact on those around us, and then in turn on others. So, make no mistake, regardless of who you are or where you live – you matter. And if we make good choices we can literally change the world. This is one of the many positives that can come out of all the uncertainty we see around us. As Gandhi famously instructed, 'Be the change you want to see in the world.' By getting our act together, you and I can be a part of the great 'change' in how we live and love, and appreciate and enjoy life. Now is the time to explore the gifts we have and nurture our self-awareness. And it all begins with 'me time'.

 It's time to see the big picture, and how much a part of the big picture you are.

What about me?

Once you begin valuing and imbuing your life with love, you will feel empowered. You will learn to create all you ever dreamed of doing, being and having, in ways that will resonate with your heart and soul. Why? Because you are exceptional. You are blessed with a deep inner knowing that has the capacity to expand your abilities far beyond your current belief systems, so allowing your dreams to become a reality.

The Wish has changed my life – it has made me more optimistic and happier about my future. Instead of being miserable, fed up and depressed, I now feel strong, optimistic and hopeful to go forward in my life. It's really changed me.
– Dee, owner of a hair salon in Paris

4

Take a quantum leap

So, let's start the Wish journey. Take yourself back to your childhood again for a moment. Recall that initial thrill of excitement, that sense of heady fulfilment. Feel its power surge through you, feel the life force moving through your whole being and out into your world. By doing this you are creating a vast positive field of glowing energy that will become a never-ending force that expands inside you, inspiring and renewing you, allowing you to make the impossible possible.

We talk a lot about power, but rarely sense what true power feels like. In this moment you are experiencing your own true power, and your imagination made it possible. Notice, as you take yourself back to the freedom of childhood, how you are suddenly liberated from your limited thinking. This is what genuine power feels like, and is another of the insights we'll be working with. True power makes us more open, more willing to reach out to others – to reconnect. But that's not all. As your life force expands and strengthens, others cannot help but notice the change taking place inside of you. Once I began to understand this principle I found friends commenting on my natural positivity, my joie de vivre, and how good it made them *feel* to be in my company.

> **True power makes us more open, more willing to reach out to others – to reconnect.**

Realise this new energy you carry is picked up and felt wherever you go. It radiates out and around you in all directions, touching your friends, your colleagues and family. There is something about you that is genuinely magnetic. It's time for you to discover the power of your true charisma. When you're a charismatic individual you will naturally draw praise, warmth and positive attention from all those you wish to have around you. Because you are one with the life force, you start to experience miracles large and small taking place in and around you, while delightful synchronicities abound, all of it empowering you even further.

As you reconnect with your own power to create, you begin to appreciate a little of what you are capable of. Steve, an insurance manager in Cardiff, tells me that when he wishes for a bus or a car parking space he creates it before starting his journey, saying he 'knows it will be there at the perfect time – it always is'. Shelley, a catering assistant in Manchester, knows that when she wants to see a movie, she only has to wish for one of her friends to ring up and offer her a ticket – and they do!

This is heady stuff, so be aware and stay calm. Your journey has only just begun and you cannot afford to become complacent when the true power of The Wish is unleashed and takes a real hold in your life.

Take a quantum leap

Therein lies the ultimate golden key of this journey: creating pure commands from planned thought by which, with the immediacy of synchronicity, opportunities then become endless and boundless.

5

Clear the road blocks

While part of you is feeling excited at the prospect of changing your life, there may well be another part that's tugging at your sleeve, telling you all these good things aren't for you – that you're dreaming, you're too flat out and exhausted trying to get through the day to do anything more, that you've got too many commitments. These things may seem true right now; however, the point is that you've reached the moment of decision. Are you going to be ruled by the patterns and issues that have made life miserable in the past, or do you want to step into the future with a brand-new vision? The choice is yours. What is it to be?

Clear the road blocks

If you're honest with yourself, you really do want a fresh start but you don't know how to make the shift. That's all right, you can do it. Take a deep breath. Relax. Now, just ask yourself what in your life so far has restricted you or is still stopping you from being the complete person you want and deserve to be? Think hard: it's not about simply saying it was your boss or mother-in-law, your bank balance or your age that has held you back.

However they have appeared or exist in your life, even these stumbling blocks can end up providing the impetus to make the change that will enable you to find the ultimate fulfilment you've always wanted but could never quite see or realise. The old adage 'one thing leads to another' rings true. That spark of realisation causes a natural alteration to take place, creating amazing opportunities through which you can evolve.

Consider these two everyday examples: attending a job interview, and going to a dinner party where you don't know anyone. As self-doubt creeps in, you'll probably expect to fluff the interview and you'd rather not go to the dinner party. But what kind of life is it when you think, 'I can't get that job, I'm not good enough' or 'No-one will speak to me at the party, I won't enjoy myself'? While these worries may loom large, these excuses are merely the same old patterns you've been creating up to now. And, if you're honest, aren't you just a tiny bit bored with them? Isn't it time you moved on?

Instead of following that old pattern of self-doubt, visualise the perfect outcome for each of the situations you are facing, how they will work out exactly as you want. This is something elite athletes do every day of the week. Think positively – remind yourself, 'I am wanted, I am loved, I am a beautiful person', as indeed you are, and *mean* it! Dismiss all that negativity and self-doubt. Tell the interviewers exactly why you're right for the job. Dazzle the other people at the dinner party with your flair. Make sure you give full rein to that burgeoning new belief in 'self', and see and feel what it can do, and is doing, for you.

Whenever those awful twinges of old worries or unhelpful self-criticism slip in to ruin any chance of enjoyment, remind yourself that these are the most destructive forces working against you, and that it's up to *you* to put them to one side. Remember that love cannot work its magic for you when such emotions are allowed to fester.

So it is time to correct all that old conditioning held deep within you by recognising that you are the only one who can change your reactions by thinking more positively about yourself. This means loving yourself, even the parts you're unsure of. When you love all parts of yourself, others will too, because they'll pick up on your energy. You deserve good things, so forgive yourself for all that's gone before, turn over a new leaf and change the rest of your life for the better. In later chapters, I'll give you a few tips on how to do this effectively.

When you love all parts of yourself, others will too, because they'll pick up on your energy.

The Wish

In the end we all can free ourselves when we start believing we are the owners of our own destiny. First, though, we have to recognise our true self, the real part of us that is filled with life and light and love. For some of us that can mean clearing away the debris of past doubts, disappointments and failures. For others it's about no longer being ruled by our fears, by what we think others expect of us, or trying to compete with people we don't even respect. All these 'aha' moments pave the way to a golden future.

6

Thoughts are wishes in disguise

Everything we see around us in the world begins with a thought, an idea, a sudden inspiration. The sudden inspirational thought that just pops into our minds when we least expect it – like inviting an old friend on an adventurous holiday, giving guidance and support to your teenage son through his exams, sorting out what to do for a friend in need or deciding how best to renovate the dreaded back bedroom – gives us the perfect opportunity to make life into something truly exciting.

On a much larger scale than the above examples, inspired thoughts have led to achievements way beyond the norm, and have been key to the creation of amazing buildings such as the Eiffel Tower and the

Taj Mahal or inventions such as the steam engine and aeroplane. All these things came from inspirational moments. So, in learning the art of wish-making, we need to keep our imaginations alive – not just for ourselves but for our children too. It is sad that even today daydreaming and flights of imagination in our children are frowned on. Yet it is our *natural* talent to daydream that will transform the unhelpful thoughts and attitudes dominating our current belief systems. To make our wishes come true we need time to daydream, to be with ourselves intimately, to make the most of 'me time'. What's more, the amount of love and attention we then give to our thought or wish will determine the extent of its creation.

> We need to keep our imaginations alive – not just for ourselves but for our children too.

From my earliest childhood my wishes would come to fruition. Admittedly some dreams, especially the big ones, took years to come about. Yet, on reflection, I can honestly say that they all came into my life. It is interesting to note that whenever I made a wish, I didn't give any thought to time: there was just this sense that it would be, whatever it was, whenever and however.

I simply believed.

When I was very young I wished for a black pony, and within a year he arrived. Bambi was four years old when he came to live with us, a mere youngster, so you could say we learned about life together. I trained him and he trained me. One day, when I was nine years old, I secretly made an intense wish – more like a vow – that I would be there with Bambi when he was old and it was his time to go. At the time I *believed* it, *saw* it and *felt* it. Thirty-five years later my wish was granted. Quite magically his passing happened on the only day in weeks that I was actually at home. Early that morning Bambi collapsed and I was there beside him, just as I had wanted to be. There was something divine about that wish that made it all possible.

The Wish

After wishing for and acquiring Bambi as a child, I progressed to a big-time wish for a magical white horse that could do amazing things like dance and leap in the air – with me riding, of course! Not surprisingly, perhaps, that wish took nearly 20 years to manifest. But manifest it did. Out of the blue an opportunity arose, a moment of pure synchronicity, for me to own such an incredible horse. One of the first sales in the world of the Lippizaner breed, the famous white dancing horses of the Vienna Riding School, was held at a venue only four miles from where I lived. For me there was no question – I knew then without any doubts whatsoever that my wish would come true. And it did. I bought a beautiful young Lippizaner, exactly the magical white dancing horse I had wished for.

As each of my wishes came to fruition, I was ecstatic – and still am – and gave deep gratitude to the universe. In a very different scenario, when I lived in central London I had to park my car on the street. Because it was in an area where incidences of car theft and vandalism were high, I would always send out a 'wish' to protect it. One morning when I was leaving for work, the police were everywhere in my street. They asked me to check my car, as ten others had been broken into, their stereos ripped out and stolen. They escorted me to my car and were amazed to discover that I hadn't lost anything – in spite of the fact that I'd forgotten to lock my car!

On another occasion my husband Andrew and I were leaving London for a week's holiday. After loading up the car he got in, leaving me to check that the house was locked. An hour or so later it dawned on me in a flash that I had left the back door to the garden wide open. There was no way I was going to tell Andrew – instead I put out the wish–thought to keep our home safe and sound. One week later we arrived home to find all just as we had left it. Andrew walked in first and was deeply alarmed and shocked to find the back door wide open – that was when I confessed!

So what does this say about wish-making? The power of belief transcends all barriers. When we *really* believe something is possible, our wish cuts through all the 'buts' and 'what ifs'. It cuts through our early conditioning, through the harsh inner critic, and brings us back to a place of wonderment and the true magic of 'being'. We return to our full potential, to all that is ours by right while we live on this earth.

This isn't just my theory, it's something an increasing number of people are experiencing, and now science is also starting to measure the results. For her book *The Intention Experiment*, Lynne McTaggart interviewed scientists, healers, Buddhist monks and Qigong masters, among others, and formulated a successful program to create the most positive results in mind-over-matter laboratory experiences. Not that I am in any way surprised: 'intention' – or, as I call it, 'wish-making' – can and does have a quantifiable scientific effect.

The question is, how can we make it work for us?

7

The power of three

Now I'd like to share with you another aspect of wish-making which can be helpful, and it's all to do with the number three. There is great power in threes. I'm sure you will have noticed how it's nearly always three wishes that the genie grants in fairy-tales, while bad luck supposedly comes along in threes as well – like buses.

Three is also the mystical number that shows up repeatedly in the great myths of the world – the Three Fates (Clotho, Lachesis and Atropos), the Three Muses (the goddesses of charm, beauty and creativity), and the Three Graces (Cephisso, Apollonis and Borysthenis, daughters of Apollo). Even Apollo's

Pythia sat on a three-legged chair (a tripod) and Cerberus was a three-headed dog. And we mustn't forget the Three Furies and the Three Gorgons as well, quite apart from surely the most famous trio of all – Caspar, Melchior and Balthasar – the Three Wise Men. Three is a prime component of folk tales, too – three little pigs, three blind mice and three bears – while the oak, ash and thorn were known as the 'fairy triad' of trees, so wherever they grew together was where the fairies lived.

Start delving deeper into threes and you begin to see just how special a number it is on many levels. Three denotes divine perfection. Three describes the eternity of Time itself through 'past', 'present' and 'future'; while 'body', 'mind' and 'spirit' encompasses Life; and 'science', 'art' and 'religion' covers pretty much everything else. All are based around three. When we throw a coin, it is generally the 'best of three' that wins. There are three primary colours, and with three we achieve geometry as well: two straight lines can never enclose a space or form a figure, nor can two flat surfaces form mass; three lines are

required for the most basic plan, and three dimensions – length, breadth and height – to form mass.

> **Start delving deeper into threes
> and you begin to see just how
> special a number it is on
> many levels.**

So the words 'good', 'better' and 'best' define our
notions of comparison and quality; while 'thought',
'word' and 'deed' describe our view of human capability;
and 'animal', 'vegetable', 'mineral' our understanding of
matter . . . The threes just go on appearing once you
start to look.

And, of course, the number three is very prevalent in nature, too. Take the bee, that hard-working
insect so vital to our well-being, for which the
number three (and its multiples) seem to be extraordinarily significant. What do I mean by this? Well,
the queen's egg takes three days to hatch, and is then
fed for nine days. It reaches maturity in 15 days,
while the worker matures in 21 days and is at work

three days after leaving its cell. The drone matures in 24 days. The bee is made up of three sections, a head and two stomachs, and its eyes are composed of some 3,000 smaller eyes, each having six sides. Underneath its body are six wax scales with which it makes the comb. The honeycomb cells each have six sides. The bee has six legs, each composed of three sections, while its feet are formed in three further triangular sections. The antennae consist of nine sections, while the sting has nine barbs on each side. Is all that by chance or design?

So why is three so prevalent? Maybe because the brain can see, count and comprehend better, quicker and easier when things – thoughts, concepts, items – are given to us in threes and no more. Go to four or beyond and it will get confused about where to look and what to look at, sending the eyes this way and that. A list of three is always going to be far easier to cope with than one of five or seven or more. So, as a child, it would make sense that all you learned was generally centred around three, at least to begin with – you had your A, B, C and your 1, 2, 3 and so on – everything in bite-size pieces, leaving little chance for confusion.

For some time I've been aware that the number three has extreme significance, and as I worked with this insight I began to see how the process of wish-making also connects to the power of three. We have already looked a little at the need to build up our life energy in order to feel empowered, to enable wishes to happen. Well, the use of threes helps us even more to create this energetic charge.

Threes figure greatly when we get into the intricacies of wish-making later in the book. In short, though, the threes are all necessary for the act of wish-creation to be properly comprehended by and fully absorbed within the brain. They give the brain something to grasp and are tangible. In considering the alchemy of wishes and wish-making, please remember three is a powerful part of this process.

8

Charge your batteries

Everything in the universe is made up of the endless movement of atoms. This movement takes energy to keep the life force moving. To enjoy movement in your life, including the desire to move forward, takes energy as well. To make wishes come true also requires life energy. So it is vital that you find positive ways of energising yourself. How do you do this?

An ancient scroll found near the Dead Sea Scrolls details three elements – thought, words and sensations – that are all absolutely vital to enable the healing process to take place effectively in the body. We have talked a little bit about feelings already, but this takes us a whole lot further. As I worked with people's emotional and physical feelings in my courses I had an even greater insight into how central they are to fulfilling our wishes. I was shown a way of working with the physical sensations we have, to alter and dispel the negative memories we hold and reinstate positive ones in their place instead. *See it, feel it, live it.*

While this may seem a little too simple, as I studied this principle I began to see just how empowering it is. It's central to making dreams come true. More than this, it works. It's worth perfecting this possibility because, make no mistake, there is a magical world all around you if you only stay still long enough to capture it.

So how does wish-making work? It comes down to your chosen words being emitted by thought in waveforms. The stronger and more focused the thought, the stronger the wave becomes, sending out signals that can be intuitively sensed and recognised by others. So when a friend is feeling miserable, they have a strong negative thought pattern, which you recognise in three ways. First, what you hear in their voice, as their tone will be lowered and inflected downward.

Second, what you see from their body language and facial expression, as their eyes will be looking down and their shoulders slumped. Third, you pick up on their depressed and needy 'energy', which affects your own energy and makes you feel like you're being sucked dry in their presence. It can even happen on the phone. Think back to a phone conversation with a deeply unhappy friend. I bet you'll remember how tired you felt afterwards. And that's why being around those who are depressed can be hard.

The opposite end of the scale is when a friend expresses great joy and excitement over something wonderful that's happened to them. Again you pick up on this in the same three ways. One, their tone will be upbeat and energised. Two, they will show physical signs of empowerment through their positive mannerisms and facial expressions: their eyes may be bright and open, their talk excited. And three, they will give off continuous positive vibes that are both energising and captivating. You will feel great being around them, and so you'll be more than happy to spend time with them.

Because your vibes can either help or hinder you,

knowing how they impact others makes it much easier for you to be positive, to have 'me time', to love and believe in yourself, and to then flourish. Your feelings are a great way to reach out to others, so you need to use them well. They're also a great barometer of what's really going on around you. Someone may seem pleasant yet you get the feeling that they don't have your best interests at heart – that they're friendly with you because you're useful to them, or because they don't have a life of their own, or because they want what you have. This is no basis for a good friendship and can drain you, even create a lot of heartache. So rather than taking people and situations at face value, listen to your feelings.

Let's look at this insight in more detail and examine how you're feeling about certain issues right now. You're going to tune into your feelings so can you get an accurate picture of where you're at.

Think about the following scenarios one at a time. First, you are going to the dentist. Second, you have booked the holiday of a lifetime. Explore how your feelings differ with each scenario.

The Wish

Concentrate on each situation for several moments to examine exactly how it really feels inside of you. Take special note of your solar plexus region, just below your chest. This is an important part of your body because it's where you hold your personal power. You can tell if the thought is a pleasurable one as it will generate a feeling of inner warmth and of positive benefit, while an unpleasant sensation will leave you feeling uncomfortable and ill at ease.

This shows you just how powerful your thoughts are, and how much they can impact on your body, either energising you and making you feel great, or making you feel unhappy and unmotivated. Remember, what you imagine you create. Good feelings have the capacity to boost your life energy, to give your wishes a head start. You can use your life energy to visualise good outcomes for yourself at work, in relationships, on holiday, in planning a reunion with old friends, or whatever else you're hoping for. It can be used to create the perfect scenario in advance, even if it's a visit to the dentist!

We'll look at the intricacies of this shortly, but first

it's vital to ensure you use your feelings positively so your energy is constantly topped up. It's not enough just to be energised, it's also important to know how to keep our energy intact and secure, so as not to lose it – we need our precious life energy to help create our most profound desires. The one region in your body that leaks energy whenever you suffer upset is, again, the solar plexus. It is the area that holds your emotions, and the more sensitive you are, the greater the loss of energy you are likely to experience through this centre.

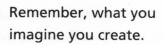 **Remember, what you imagine you create.**

Here's a brilliant little exercise to ensure you look after your energy. Use it regularly and it will benefit you enormously.

First, stand up, take a breath in, let it go, and smile. Bring your hands together in front of your thighs, with your fingers extended and only your fingertips

The Wish

touching those of the opposite hand. Keep your
hands a couple of inches away from your body.

Still with your fingertips touching and your hands
a few inches from your body, move your hands slowly
and deliberately up the front of your body, up to your
mouth, and then take them apart, drawing each
hand away on either side of your face. It's just like
doing up a zip – which is exactly what you're doing
to seal in and protect your energy! You can do this
little exercise in the morning before going out, or at
any time you feel the need, say before a meeting or
a date. It will stop anyone taking your energy from
you and weakening you mentally, physically or
emotionally. That means more energy for creating the
perfect climate for your zest for life.

One of the most important things I do now is to zip
up my energy. I've become very aware of not absorbing people's negative energy or being drained by
them, so I'm now very good at putting up the
protection shields and keeping my own energy so that
I'm more useful too . . . I've been much happier, much

Charge your batteries

more positive and have a stronger belief in myself –
you're looking after yourself really, rather than always
absorbing everything going on around you.

– Jenny, human resources manager, London

9

Why your words matter

Now we've looked at your feelings and their importance to your life energy, it's time to take a look at the effect of words. Words hold immense power and are an essential part of helping our wishes come true, but how can we use them in an empowering way?

You need to take the initiative to make your wish a reality. This may seem obvious but what we're talking about is initiating the thought-command to literally make your wish happen. You make this command by putting the right words together. It's all about the detail – never leave anything to chance when you are making a wish.

Words hold immense power and are an essential part of helping our wishes come true.

How does this work? When you enjoy a sense of inner happiness, you naturally feel alive and energised. It is a spark of this energy that lights up your mind and gives you the perfect moment to work with your thought, to command that what you dream of will take place. When you form the right words for your wish, the energy behind your words will then expand and, like a magnetic field, attract to you what is needed, so that you can confidently find your new job, write your book, travel overseas, take up study or whatever else you'd love to do. By choosing the right words, your full potential – that has been waiting in the wings – comes alive like a Formula One racing car, accelerating hard off the grid.

When you command the power of your 'thought-intention' mentally and visually, and at the same time feel the sensation of anticipation we looked at earlier, you help create your future path. Our words then make our thoughts and feelings – and our wishes – more concrete. But before we can add the power of words into the mix, it's important we balance those thoughts and feelings. For example, some of us may have come across people who have great difficulty in feeling – let alone showing – emotions because they have lost the sensibility to do so. Others are so emotional they have trouble controlling their feelings. If our thoughts or feelings are unbalanced, it's almost impossible to be proactive.

Take Fay, a highly successful woman in finance, who phoned me in a terrible state because she'd just lost her job. Fay had been with the company for more than ten years and the redundancy came out of the blue. Her employer simply gave her four weeks' wages and asked her to leave the same day. The shock of it was devastating to her. Fay took it personally and suddenly felt completely useless, and also betrayed by the company to which she had given so much of her life. I assured her that the business viewpoint is never personal and that the cold, calculating way she was sacked is driven by economics, not compassion – I should know, I used to work in the corporate sector. For Fay to move on, I had to help her forget the emotion of losing her job and instead focus on how she was going to bring her own empowerment back to its full potential.

When we suffer any kind of shock, it understandably takes time to recover, so it is essential to start the process of rebuilding one's 'self' as quickly as possible. I often suggest taking time out for a few days, maybe staying with friends, even taking a holiday – it makes all the difference when you go away somewhere: you view things through differently coloured glasses. What we need is (yes, you've got it) 'me time'! We need to be reminded of who we are, above and beyond the dramas we're facing. Why? Because this brings us back to centre. It is only then that we will find how best to move forward. Should it be a close friend or family member and not you who has the problem, remind yourself that you can't live their life for them but you can assist them on their journey – when asked.

The Wish

Words can help us with this rebalancing process. Like many of us, what Fay needed was daily word-commands to reinstate her power. In Fay's case, I told her to say, **'I am the power, I am in charge of my life, I am safe'** three times every morning and evening for two weeks – this was her 'word-command'. After only ten days the change in her was immense. When she came back to see me her mood was very positive and upbeat, and she had even made the decision not to do the same type of job again, sent out her résumé and already had several exciting potential work offers. Another week went by, and then she called me and said, 'Guess what? I have a new job, with more money and far less stress.'

Remember, when facing a problem, use creative thinking with word-commands – in other words, go outside the box. Use your intention (in other words, focus your thoughts) to work through the issue, and then use your intuition – your inspiration – to find the right word-command to help you reclaim your power and so create the desired outcome. When you use your words well, you will then be able to do something quite exceptional and unusual.

You can also use words in the most practical of ways, as Sean and his friends did when they needed to catch a plane. 'We wanted to know that tomorrow – the twenty-third – would be a good day to fly,' he told me. 'So we put out our wish that it would be a good day to fly, even though there were more than 100 people on the waiting list. Then, against all likelihood, we got a call from the airline saying that all four of us were confirmed to travel on the twenty-third. There's a wonderful feeling about being in sync with the universe!' Sean's thought-commands were clear, so the universe was able to respond.

The same was true for Sunny, an Australian girl in her late twenties working in London, who told me she was going for a really fantastic job but was worried it didn't pay as much money as she was already earning. Sunny explained that she didn't want to sound money-driven to her prospective employers, but she believed that she was worth more than they were offering. Sunny found it difficult to say what she wanted, so I suggested for the three days before her interview she worked on her thoughts. This involved her sitting

61

quietly for a few moments each day and saying three times the thought-command 'I am worth £3000 a month'. This was the figure she wanted but was frightened to say. Three days later, when the interviewer asked her what salary she wanted, Sunny stated the £3000 figure with total confidence. Two days later she was offered the job and with it the salary she had asked for.

When we're clear with our thoughts, it's much easier for the universe to respond in kind. Words help us join the dots and make our wishes happen.

10

Who am I?

We've already looked at the value of 'me time', but now it's time to give yourself a much-needed boost of confidence by finding out more about who you actually are. Have you any idea who that really is? This is a major question to answer, yet most of us simply continue to rush through our daily routine unaware that the expectations we have of ourselves stem from our family, culture or background, from our work or friends, from where we live, or from advertising and popular culture, rather than from our own self-knowledge.

When we think about who we are, most of us will automatically think of our name, as that's how we identify ourselves. This makes sense as words hold great power. They capture something essential about a person, place or object. When you give this some thought, you realise your name does indeed say something about you. The numerous books on names and their historical, cultural and linguistic meanings show just how important names are.

The meanings behind your name offer another way of recognising who you are. My name simply comes from 'angel' and to me signifies a messenger. How appropriate is that? So take a moment to consider your own name. (A name, however, can also disguise your identity and thus fail to represent who you feel you are. A friend told me that when she was very young she could not and would not use her given name, Janine. She kept telling her parents that her 'true' name was Sasha, and started to use it from then on. She kept it, too, convinced it was the only name truly appropriate to her.)

There's a wonderfully empowering technique you can use to align yourself with the true essence of your name, where you sound out your name like a mantra in quiet moments – in the car, the shower, your bedroom. This strengthens the energetic field, stops you feeling you have to apologise for yourself, and puts you in contact with the essential you.

Having thought about your name and what it reveals about you, it's time to dig a little deeper into who you are by looking at what you love doing. Take a piece of paper and list as many things as you can about what you like to do. It doesn't matter how simple each thing is, or even if it's something you've only done once in your life. Write it down, because each point holds a key to your happiness. And don't stop at one or two items – keep the ideas flowing until you've exhausted your list of things that make life special in some way.

Now take a moment to look over all the things you've written down. Notice how good it feels to think about all the life-enhancing possibilities you have before you. So, what do you do with it?

When I first did this for myself I suddenly realised that if I were to make some room for the many wonderful possibilities I'd listed, there'd be little or no time left for doing the mundane bits, the very dullest things in our lives. Of course, we still have to pay the bills, buy the groceries, clean the house and do a whole range of things that help maintain us and our families, but that doesn't have to be the focal point of the day or week.

Inspired by my list, I started rearranging my days and weeks to allow more time for the work that I enjoy and for the things I love to do in my spare time – for me this meant riding my horse, cooking a special meal, meeting an old friend for a catch-up dinner, arranging a party, and planning a trip.

By doing what we love, what feeds us, we elevate our life energy – just like we did when we thought about our wishes coming true. The more we do this, the more we live in a happier space, making it far easier to attract more of the same. The higher our life energy, the less effort it takes to draw good things to us.

The next step is to carve out some very special time to enjoy just 'being' or, more importantly, doing what we love. For example, the harassed exec might decide that, whatever his workload, he's going to take charge and leave work on time that day, and go on to have a great evening out. The busy mum might schedule her day differently to stop running on the same old rails – perhaps someone else can pick up the kids for a change!

When we love what we do, we put all our enthusiasm into our projects and then it's not at all difficult for us to be involved, engaged, dynamic. This is why 'me time' is one of the major keys to finding fulfilment. Actually inviting these special moments into our lives is a huge step forward and quite an achievement. Whether it's by relaxing, planning something exciting or just doing something wholly different, simply taking a few moments to find out more about your real self is an amazing leap forward – especially for those who haven't struck out in this way before. While for some of you it may indeed seem a luxury, remember it is one you truly deserve. None of us can afford to miss or ignore any opportunity for increased well-being, fulfilment, and to find our true self.

Finding out what makes your heart sing is without doubt the path to happiness and contentment. Sadly, though, often these qualities are lacking from every-day life. What you generate from within will have a great effect on all those around you. When you do what you love, you impact on other people's lives in all kinds of unexpected ways. Suppose someone says something extremely complimentary to you in passing. If you feel good about yourself, you may well smile and thank them, and allow their compliment to give you a wonderful confidence boost and a real feeling of self-worth. This in turn will flow on and benefit the next person you speak to or smile at, whether you're in the supermarket or filling the car with gas. You will light up their day, and they will end up doing the same thing for someone else, and so on. There's no end to the good we can create when we're true to doing what we love.

Finding out what makes your heart sing is without doubt the path to happiness and contentment.

Who am I?

A gentle piece of advice: not everyone will respond as you'd hoped, but that's part of the process of becoming clear about yourself and not allowing others to run your life. There are those who certainly don't want you to become a fully self-empowered and wholly independent person. Why? Because then they would have no hold over you. They may be insecure friends, a difficult boss, a close relative or even a partner. Knowing that you have someone in your life who stifles you can make you feel hurt or fearful, because you worry about making changes that will rock the boat. Don't let any of this get to you; it may just be your get-out-of-jail card.

The greatest way to change the world is to start by changing your *self* from within. And as you begin knowing more and thinking more for yourself, you will become a self-fulfilling prophecy of who you most want to be.

Remember, when you grow within, you become a better person and by extension the world becomes a better place. A good way to move forward when you're feeling a bit wobbly is to ask the Source of the

Universe for assistance. This is our greatest link to our Creator, where Love is boundless and we are able to receive for our highest and greatest good. Then step out on your own journey of self-discovery.

> As you begin knowing more
> and thinking more for yourself,
> you will become a self-fulfilling
> prophecy of who you most
> want to be.

11

Live your passion

Having made your list of what you love doing and thought about how best to carve out some 'me time', let's hone this process. No-one may have told you before that you have the power to create – but it is all within you. This is a big thought, so take a moment to let it sink in. The key to creation is having the energy available to make it happen. We've looked at the importance of love, and now it's time to examine your passions, but how do they fit together? Love is the foundation of all wish-making, and passion is what gets the thought moving. To spark your passion you need to have boundless energy at your disposal.

Love is the foundation of all wish-making, and passion is what gets the thought moving.

When you are passionate about something and you share that with others, it spills out and radiates all around you. It is picked up and felt by everyone. The effect can be astounding. Passion helps attract success and fulfilment. Time and again I have listened to company directors saying things like 'She was so passionate about her work, which is why I gave her the contract.' When you speak with true passion, it comes through in your tone of voice, your mannerisms and the sheer joy with which you talk. It's the real thing and people instinctively grasp this. Or as someone once said, 'To be successful you must have 90 per cent energy and 10 per cent talent.'

This is not to belittle talent in any way, but this person knew very well that the energy required for success has to be boundless. Talent is a given, but you need ever-expanding enthusiasm throughout your life for lift-off.

Live your passion

This is a world away from getting lost in all those mundane issues that in most cases only seem to drain us. Why do they have this effect? Because we are not passionate about them. When we're imprisoned by our 'to do' lists, we miss out on all the wonderful things life offers. How many times have you been invited out only to say you can't go because you've got to get the car fixed, look after the kids, do your hair, go to a parents' meeting, start on the accounts, walk the animals, fix the back door, or whatever?

Which all goes back to the importance of creating a few moments for yourself and feeling worthy enough to spend a little time on what you actually enjoy, something you are passionate about. It could be seeing a film, having a meal at your favourite restaurant, reading a book you've been looking forward to – the crucial thing is that it's important to *you*.

When you're passionate you're more able to prioritise, to do all the maintenance stuff with ease, because you're motivated to get out and have a life. It also helps you say yes to the things that are good for you, and to pass on the things that are not. As you learn how to fully enjoy everyday life, you will benefit quite naturally from many small inspirational moments that result from following your passions and which can in turn dramatically boost your energy and give you greater confidence.

This shift is a profound effect just waiting to be realised. It is an ever-increasing field made up of effort, enthusiasm and passion, where 'effort' is self-motivation and 'enthusiasm' is inner excitement. So while it takes 'effort' to get out of bed in the morning and 'enthusiasm' to organise an event, couple both with 'passion' – the love that boosts all you do – and you create a powerful dynamic for everyday living. And when all three come alive and sing in unison in all you start doing in your life, your life will never be the same again.

In writing down my passions for the first time, I became aware of what I truly loved and wanted to do in my life: I now know I can use these within my career.

– Shelley, caterer, Manchester and London

Live your passion

So how do you learn who you are and become aware of all you have to offer? Try the following exercise.

First, grab a paper and pen, find somewhere quiet and comfortable, a place where you won't be disturbed, and switch off your phone. Sit upright, but keep your feet on the ground – this is important as it helps you to stay earthed and to consciously direct your attention.

Say these words to yourself: 'I am calm, prepared and ready.' (You can also use this phrase whenever you need to relax and feel safe.)

Next, write your first name at the top of a page, and spend several moments thinking about your name – this is you, after all!

Take a few moments to think about what your main passions are. When you're ready, make a list of your top ten passions, numbering them in order from one to ten, with one being your greatest passion. These don't have to be things you've done in the past, or things you'd enjoy doing if you only had the time – it's what you would do when your greatest wish came true. So it's important when writing down your passions that you don't dismiss things because you can't realistically see them happening. Write this list from your heart, the centre of all your beautiful passion.

Be conscious of any moments of doubt or fear while you're making your list. If you're experiencing any of these 'blocks', remind yourself that it is only your belief system that's kicking in. Simply put all that nagging negative chatter aside and focus on those things that make you happy. Joyful thoughts strengthen your body, and even your immune system, and focusing on them makes it much easier to gain greater self-empowerment and balance, enabling your wishes to come true.

Your passions will elevate you to a new way of understanding. To assist you in acknowledging and recognising your own passions, consider the following examples of different types of pleasures:

Live your passion

1 Physical pleasures: Dancing, singing, football, swimming, walking, cooking, shopping, working with animals.

2 Mental pleasures: reading, communicating, writing, painting, negotiating, organising, promoting, analysing, working with other people.

3 Emotional pleasures: music, acting, art, films.

4 Spiritual pleasures: creative thought, conscious awareness, happiness, meditation, relaxation, prayer.

Now let's have a closer look at who you really are.

Look at your list of top ten passions. The first three you listed are the most significant as they are the true 'you'. They will be the ones to give you complete satisfaction and enjoyment. They have the capacity to strongly boost your success whether in work or at home. Whatever role you now choose in life should include the top three.

Look again at the first three passions listed. You can move them around if you wish. These three entries have the power to change your life. Once you recognise them, use them within your daily life and

your career, because they link you to your talents and
true purpose.

How remarkable to have this insight! Keep this list
at hand, as your passions will directly link you to
your role in life, your *true purpose* for living and
being here at this time.

12

Put your fears under the microscope

While our passions empower us beyond anything we can imagine, often we don't embrace them because we're full of fear. Let's face it, fear is a big one for most of us, especially at this time – wherever you look, the world seems to be full of fear, and many people are intent on instilling even more fear within us. If we took what we see on the news and read in the papers as the total picture of what's happening daily on the planet, then it would be almost impossible to feel positive enough to get out of bed in the morning. And if we believed the multimillion-dollar ad campaigns, we'd be convinced we're nothing without the latest must-have branded item or that no-one will love us if we have wrinkles.

The Wish

Before you move forward you need to be aware of what is cutting you off from becoming all you truly are and want to be. One of the difficulties is that fear is held in our subconscious mind and can sabotage us in all kinds of ways we're not aware of unless we know our true selves well. I call the subconscious brain the 'toolbox', as it carries all the tools necessary to survive in our physical body, encompassing our instincts, physical body, sex drive, intellect, emotions and imagination. When we use any of these areas of our life without being conscious of what we're doing, we can come unstuck – and often this is where our deepest fears come in. We may fill our lives with sex, because we're afraid we're unlovable or we're too scared to commit in any other way. Our emotions may rule our lives because we never stop to think about what we're doing, we just react. We may find it impossible to make things happen for ourselves because we find real life scary and prefer to live in a fantasy world. We need to unpack our fears, so they don't continue to prevent us from being the complete person we want to be.

Put your fears under the microscope

Often we run a mile from our fears. But when we face and work with them, we place ourselves back in the driver's seat, as Anthony, a successful financial trader based in Geneva, discovered. When Anthony realised his greatest stumbling block was his fear of heights, he saw how it had caused him insurmountable problems in other areas of his life; his fear affected his ability to enjoy the things he loved, including travelling. Anthony decided to confront this fear of heights, and after completing The Wish he felt strong enough to go and test his newfound empowerment – to 'know' his fear. A couple of months later he took a trip to a bridge in Zurich known as the 'suicide bridge'. He walked right across that bridge and back without a problem.

You may actually know the real source of your fears because it's lying dormant in your memories. Fear often arises in the strangest ways. It can be triggered by any of our senses, even a smell or taste, which can activate an unpleasant memory. Say, for example, that when you were a young child the neighbour's dog bit you while you were patting it.

That memory would naturally come flooding back any time you see a dog, so you become scared of dogs. I remember at my first school the food was quite disgusting and there was one weekly meal – shepherd's pie – that used to make me feel sick, but we were made to eat it. Since then, anytime I smell shepherd's pie it brings back those bad memories of my school days, and I purposely avoid or rush past the area where the smell is coming from. Your subconscious mind or 'toolbox' contains all your memories, good, bad and indifferent. Bad memories, if unresolved, remain as your fears and can trigger the self-doubt that will disempower you.

Now, though, you are going to recognise and understand your fears. This is one of the most powerful exercises we'll be doing together. It will help your self-empowerment in very real and lasting ways. Basically, once you have your fears nailed, there's nothing you can't accomplish. In his inaugural speech during the height of the Great Depression, President Roosevelt reminded the American people that in spite of the huge challenges of massive unemployment and poverty, 'The only thing we have to fear is fear itself – nameless, unreasoning, unjustified terror which paralyzes needed efforts to convert retreat into advance.'

> **Once you have your fears nailed, there's nothing you can't accomplish.**

So how do you move forward and turn your fears into excitement? You start by accepting them for what they were – a past experience with no present-day reality. In recognising and understanding this, you start taking your power back, and in accepting this truth, the real *you* will, in no time at all, be in control.

Let me explain. Your consciousness links you and your Soul to the Source of the Universe. It is well described as your 'true will'. Our true will is 'the ability to act or refrain from acting at any one time'. This means that when you create a command it is directed into action by your will. So the whole power of your wish comes from your *conscious* command.

The Wish

Your 'toolbox' or subconscious helps as well by providing you with the imagination to make a wish in the first place.

A quick word: not all fear is bad. Instinctive fear is built into our psyche and is very much a part of being human. It tells us when danger is near and alerts us to the 'fight or flight' reaction we have when we're in an emergency or being attacked. It makes us cautious when we're out alone late at night, if we're approached by suspicious strangers, or even if we're driving through a thunderstorm.

Let's have a look at the fears that are currently running your life. Make a list of them. Keep to a maximum of five and then number them in order, with number one as your worst fear. Again, don't get into analysis paralysis, just write them down.

Writing down your fears is a significant moment, because as you look at your list you can see the elements in your life that are holding you back. So far your fears have taken every opportunity to block your highest and greatest potential for success and happiness. From now on you are going to be in charge and start making conscious decisions about what you want in your life.

Take a look at what you've written down. If you have more than one fear, you may find your fears are interrelated. Anthony listed his fears as 'loss of purpose', 'humiliation', 'isolation', 'vertigo', 'lack of control' and 'perfectionism'. As he looked at these fears he came to realise they all revolved around his father, a perfectionist, who had quietly expected his son to be perfect as well. So, as an adult, when Anthony felt he was out of control and without proper purpose, he believed he had failed. His self-worth was virtually nil. Once he worked with The Wish he found out where his real passions lay. His confidence grew in leaps and bounds and, with it, his self-esteem. He no longer needed to be perfect.

Realise that fear is also the absence of 'knowing'. Acknowledging, accepting and understanding your fears gives you power over them. Once you understand this and hold onto this 'knowing', your fear is corrected and dissolves.

The Wish

(If you can't find the memory from events in your early days, it may be from a past-life memory. Yes, it is possible! In such instances I would advise you to consider seeking a psychotherapist who specialises in past-life regression and healing, and work through it with them.)

Now let's look at some fear connections which may well be destroying you with self-doubt. See if you have written any of these words in your list of fears:

Loss – commitment – isolation – imprisonment – abandonment – suppression

These are all signs of unfulfilment, reflecting a sense of inner loneliness. This is perhaps the most common fear, which then triggers a terrible sense of foreboding, blocking your future. Carol, for example, had a continual fear that she was going to be alone. She had never given any thought to where her fear came from, until she uncovered a memory of a time when her mother had walked out and left her. Carol now realised she was re-creating her past and thus making it into her future.

Put your fears under the microscope

Poverty – failure – humiliation – criticism – lack of
achievement – guilt – confrontation – self-doubt
All these make us feel totally helpless and vulnerable,
and until we build our own strengths through
understanding what has happened to us in the past,
we will continue to suffer. Sue was a very successful
IT expert yet she still, seemingly irrationally, feared
failure and poverty – until she remembered being
told by her teacher at primary school that she was
useless and a failure. It had stayed buried in her life,
blocking her. To help her overcome these fears, Sue
said an affirmation to herself for two weeks: 'I am
worthy, I love myself, I am now in charge of my life.'
And now she is.

Poor health – pain – disability – insanity – death
Please do not think you are alone if you fear one or
more of these. Very few people can say they
haven't had an early experience linking them to
these fears, usually involving a much-loved family
member or close friend. That type of held memory
will disempower you more quickly than most and

The Wish

leave you without a sense of identity. Jane came to me quite recently and told me her number one fear was of insanity. It turned out her mother had suffered dementia and had been in a home for years. When Jane fully understood her own power and turned the fear around, she succeeded in creating major changes in her life. Amazed, she started living again.

Fire – water – flying – heights – animals – attack
More often than not there is a dormant memory here of some unpleasant event taking place when you were young. It could be one you buried deep down as it is just too frightening to give it thought. Kate, a dear friend, told me she had a terrible fear of fire. When she looked back and gave herself the time – and the strength – to think about it, she remembered her hands being burnt when she put them too close to the hearth when she was very little. Then she relived the experience with me, and calmly reinstated and changed the encounter with a wonderful feeling of protection and safety. It worked.

Put your fears under the microscope

Now that you understand more of the shape and meaning of your fears, close your eyes and think for a moment about your number one, your very worst fear. Look deep inside you and re-run it . . . It's all right, you are in charge, you are safe. Think of it as just like watching a short but scary movie.

As you are doing this, take a breath in and let it go, then tell yourself: 'I am safe, I understand and release my fear for good.' Say this three times to implant it strongly as a command. Then take a breath, let it go, relax and SMILE. Repeat this affirmation three times whenever you feel the need – it will empower you, turning any fear into a feeling of excitement instead. Now you have faced your fears you will already be feeling a greater strength within you.

Here's a brilliant hint to assist you whenever that old fear tries to slip back into your mind. Use the words in the above affirmation – 'I am safe, I understand and release my fear for good' – and at the same time snap your middle finger and thumb together once. It acts as a really powerful control switch, obliterating that niggling fear coming from your toolbox. I do it whenever I need to and it works every time.

Often people tell me that they began their particular journey of discovery due to a crisis – this always makes me smile, as it seems somehow so appropriate that we 'summon' a crisis into our lives. By that I mean the crisis has been called in by our soul intelligence, the all-seeing, all-knowing part of us that draws to us everything we need to be truly empowered. It helps us see the gifts in even the most difficult moments so that ultimately no experience is ever lost.

Years ago Jan came to work for me to look after my horses. She was a sensitive person and had a wonderful way with animals. Jan was in an unhappy marriage. She had been praying for a way out but didn't have the courage to actually leave her husband. One day while riding in the hills, Jan passed a lone man walking with his dog. They did not speak, she just rode past him. Later, quite suddenly, her horse got spooked and reared. Jan fell backwards off the rearing horse and it fell on top of her, trapping them both in a deep ditch. Jan was pinned underneath, unconscious.

By now the man was wondering why he couldn't see the woman who'd ridden past him a little earlier. He had a clear view of the hills around him, yet he couldn't see her or her horse. Knowing she couldn't have just disappeared, he was concerned enough to go back to check. He found Jan and her horse, and urgently called for help.

Jan was in hospital for almost a year. She learned to walk again – even though the doctors said she would never be able to. After her accident and all those months of rehabilitation, Jan regained her own empowerment and realised how wonderful it was to be herself and to be able to make her own decisions – she had got her life back. Jan told me later with great delight that when her husband eventually turned up to take her home, 'I felt so empowered I told him exactly what I thought of him and where to go – and I've never looked back since.'

Your own newfound knowledge of what your fears

are and why they have been major players in your life up to now brings freedom that will elevate you to your greatest potential and take you to those dizzy heights where your dreams can turn into wishes that come true.

13

Your unique role in life

Now that you know your passions, and understand your fears and have given them the kicking they so richly deserve, let's find out what your talents truly are. When you know where your true talents lie, you're able to work them into your daily life, giving yourself the opportunity to find complete fulfilment.

Each and every one of us is unique and each of us has a special role in life. In my case it was my heightened intuitive ability to see, hear and feel through telepathy to benefit all those around me with messages of hope. However, I fought this calling for years, believing I should be running a business and becoming a mega-career woman! Now, though, I can say that, yes, I am extremely good at what I do: it has become part of my special role in life.

> **Each and every one of us is unique and each of us has a special role in life.**

Some of you may be close to knowing what your true role is, others may feel they have no idea what they're meant to be doing with their life. But when you know you are in the right place at the right time – or indeed, when you know where you need to be to make it happen – you, too, can experience the sheer enjoyment that comes from finding your special role in life, to do whatever it is that encompasses all you have to offer when your talents are properly and fully recognised.

Just imagine for a moment that you are living, breathing and working with your greatest talent – and how that feels. Your energy increases and you feel empowered to do your life's work. Only now it isn't like 'work' at all, is it? Whether you're a shop assistant, fashion designer, gardener, bank clerk or doctor, when you're concentrating on and doing what you truly want, you don't care what anyone else thinks, says or expects of you. You are happy.

So when we talk about 'talents', what do we mean? Obviously, our talents can be very many things, from having a great eye for detail or a way with words, to an ability to connect with animals. Perhaps you love inspiring and motivating people, or you feel empathy when they have problems. Or you could be very good at drawing or painting, or maybe it's sports you excel in. The list is endless, as it covers anything you feel you have a gift or talent for.

To discover what your talents are, try this exercise.

Take a pen and paper and find a comfortable place to sit somewhere quiet. Now, write a list of your talents, the things that you know you are good at. Keep it to a maximum of ten.

When you're done, look at what you have written and decide which are your top three. These three talents point you towards what you are meant to be doing in life. When you acknowledge and act upon your greatest talents, and they become a part of your career and your life's work, you will vastly increase your overall well-being and self-confidence.

Now that you have your top three talents, go back to your top three passions and write them down together.

Think about your unique blend of passions and talents. As you begin to absorb them, what does it tell you about yourself? This is a really crucial insight, so take a moment to understand and absorb the knowledge of what is being shown to you. Knowing where your talents and passions meet is seriously empowering because it enables you to find your 'real' identity, your true purpose for living and being here at this time.

Sally, for example, had a financially successful career in advertising, but she felt she wasn't in the right job, and as a result her life seemed unfulfilled. Using this exercise, she listed her top three talents as 'organising', 'motivating' and 'negotiating', while her top three passions were 'assisting others', 'entertaining' and 'travel'. After thinking about her talents and passions, Sally decided to look for a job that utilised both what she was good at and what she loved. Six months later she started a new career as an international event organiser. And guess what? She loves her new role and using her talents in a much more exciting, rewarding and fulfilling way.

So let's take a moment to consolidate what you've learned about yourself and your wonderful unique powers. First, stand up, take a breath, let it go, and smile. Now say three times, **'My role in life gives me complete self-worth.'** And don't just say the words – think about them, mean them.

Keep doing this affirmation for two to three days, or more if necessary, to let it sink in. It always works when it's in line with your inner truth, and quite naturally you will feel a great sense of achievement, inner power and knowing. Congratulate yourself – you have now become fully empowered to progress in your life.

The Wish

There's one affirmation I use regularly – 'Love and trust feed my energy field.' I say it three times every morning and feel much more power in my body physically. It actually empowers me, kind of shifts something, shifts any doubt about life or who I am.

– **Richard, film director, London**

14

What has DNA got to do with it?

In these pages you are taking a close look at who you are, so it's important to go to the very core of what resonates within you physically. This is your DNA, or deoxyribonucleic acid, the blueprint for your life.

DNA is found in all living things. In human beings, more than 99 per cent of our DNA sequence is the same. The tiny percentage that isn't the same is what makes you the unique person you are – your hair colour, your height and so on. That's why DNA has become so important in crime investigations. It's estimated that if you could unwrap all the DNA in your body, you'd be able to reach from the Earth to the moon six thousand times. Our genes are made of pieces of DNA. Genes are passed down from our parents and contain a lot of information about our ancestry.

DNA is exciting stuff! Let me tell you of an amazing experiment carried out by the Institute of HeartMath in Boulder Creek, California, which I believe makes my points for me. In this experiment (Modulation of DNA Conformation by Heart-focused Intention, 1993) researchers monitored and measured the effects of emotions on human placenta DNA, the most pristine DNA form there is. The DNA was placed in a phial where any changes could be measured and this was handed to 28 researchers who had each been trained to generate strong emotions.

The experiment discovered that the DNA actually changed its shape according to the researchers' feelings! For example, when the researchers felt gratitude, love and joy, the DNA responded by relaxing its strands, unwinding them to become longer. And when the researchers felt fear, anger, frustration and stress, the DNA shortened and tightened up, in turn switching off many DNA codes. So if you've ever felt 'shut down' by your negative emotions, this is why. Such 'shut-downs' were simply reversed, however, when the researchers felt feelings of love, gratitude and joy again.

But the experiment didn't stop there. The institute later performed a follow-up experiment with HIV-positive patients. They discovered that feelings of love, joy, gratitude and appreciation increased immune resistance by 300,000 times: it seems clear from this that if you keep feelings of joy, love and gratitude in your heart and life, you are less likely to let viruses, flu or bacteria break through your immune system and get you down.

So now we know a little more about DNA, but you might be wondering, what's DNA got to do with wish-making? A lot, actually. In fact, understanding – and healing – your DNA can help you reinstate your 'true' self and reach your full potential.

Many people believe they have been disadvantaged by the genes passed down to them by their parents. Veronica, for example, was convinced she would suffer the same thyroid problem her mother had, while David questioned whether he would die of a sudden heart attack, just as his father and great-grandfather had. Sound familiar?

Understanding – and healing – your DNA can help you reinstate your 'true' self and reach your full potential.

While it's true that some illnesses are inherited, and there is no replacement for medical treatment, it is possible to heal your own DNA. I'm going to show you a wonderful technique that uses the power of thought to harmonise and realign the memory coding of your DNA. Working on your DNA can help you to feel stronger, calmer, happier, more energised and fully attuned, and this in turn will help you to make your wishes happen.

One of the best ways to work on this fundamental part of yourself is to use the following visualisation technique. Don't panic if you aren't able to visualise, you can simply talk yourself through the exercise instead – what matters is your *intention* to bring about needed change, so stay gently but firmly focused on your DNA and this technique will still work for you.

The double helix of DNA looks a bit like two entwined snakes. Note the 'rungs' in the double helix, the gentle curve of the strands. It's remarkable to think you're looking at the building blocks of life itself.

When you feel you have a good sense of what DNA looks like, get a pen and paper and find somewhere quiet to sit where you won't be disturbed. Remember to turn off that phone and shut any doors or windows so you can be in your own space. Now relax.

As you allow yourself to feel relaxed, look at the diagram again; see it as an example of your DNA structure.

Now, draw your own DNA. Immerse yourself in your drawing. Enjoy the experience. Make sure you take the whole page to do this. Don't get caught up in trying to be perfect: this isn't about drawing the DNA exactly, it's just your way of describing your

DNA. If you wish to add colours, then do so – it's up to you.

Slowly take a breath in, and let it go. Do this three times, then tell yourself to relax. Close your eyes and feel the calm radiating through your body.

Next, imagine there is a cinema-sized screen in front of you with a bright blue frame all round it. In your mind, put the image of perfect DNA on the screen. Tell yourself it is there exactly as it is drawn in the diagram. Once it's up on the screen, see the strands moving in a liquid motion and say, 'This is my DNA.'

Turn the DNA strands into a gently moving golden fluid – literally liquid gold. See the beautiful gold moving all through your DNA strands. Tell yourself this liquid gold is now in your body. Feel this healing gold permeate every strand of your DNA, every atom, every fibre of your being. You may feel a sudden warmth or tingling, or you might feel a little more optimistic or an unexpected thrill of excitement. Whatever your response, enjoy it, as you've done something truly significant here.

Now tell yourself, 'My DNA is now in perfect working order. It is healed and I now have optimum health.' Say this three times.

Notice how you are feeling. Then, when you're ready, take a breath in and let it go. Smile and open your eyes.

This powerful visualisation technique is one of the keys to the wish-forming process. Using this exercise, you can make a significant change take place in your body for optimum health, while clearing out the old resonating memories.

Some of you may find that the residue of past ailments or health issues can actually be felt for a short time afterwards. Within an hour of completing the DNA exercise, Dan suddenly felt the recurrence of the pain he experienced when he broke his leg as a child. Do not worry if this happens to you – this is all good news as your DNA is literally throwing out the residue that had been festering away inside you for years, clearing it once and for all. Just sit for a few moments and say these words to yourself: **'I am now** in perfect balance, I release all residual memories, I release them to the universe.' Say this three times. Take a breath in and let it go.

While it's likely you will be feeling strange new sensations, or have inspirational thoughts coming into your conscious mind, it is all wonderfully positive and part of the spiritual transformation that is taking place within. You are taking charge of your 'toolbox' and becoming empowered. Well done!

15

Time to balance

One of the crucial aspects of successful wish-making is getting yourself into balance. Already you've learned about the importance of love and passion, of healing your DNA and overcoming your fear, in order to enhance your life energy. You now know how to seal your energy so that it's not leaking out all over the place. Now you need to beneficially balance yourself, so you can further enhance your ability to attract good into your life.

This exercise will help you find balance in all areas of your life and strengthen any areas where you are weak. Make sure that you do each step of the exercise before reading on.

The Wish

Get a pen and paper and get ready to draw. Then, without giving it too much thought, draw circles to represent each of the four key aspects of your life – mental, physical, emotional and spiritual. The circles don't have to be the same size; you can draw them as big or as little as you like. You should now have four circles each with a word in them – a physical circle, a mental circle and so on.

When you're done, look at your circles. Some of you may find that your circles are all about the same size – if so, that's great news, as you are already balanced in all areas of your life. However, most of us will find that the sizes of our circles vary. I have noticed, for example, that women tend to draw bigger emotional and spiritual circles, while men draw bigger mental and physical circles.

Look at which circle you have made the smallest and give it a tick. This will be the one you need to work on, as it is currently your weakest zone.

If your 'physical' circle is the smallest, then it's likely your body has been suffering ailments and is lacking energy. When Caroline first did this exercise, she drew a tiny physical circle: at the time she was recovering from a bout of flu. She worked on eating healthily and taking care of herself for a few weeks, then did the exercise again. This time when she drew her physical circle, it had expanded because she felt stronger and better.

If, like Caroline, you discover that your lack of balance is due to physical weakness, try the following affirmation. Sit somewhere comfortable in a relaxed state with your eyes closed and say, 'Love and trust feed my energy field.' Say the affirmation three times daily for up to two weeks – you'll be amazed how much stronger you become in that short period of time.

If your 'mental' circle is the smallest, start using your mind more to expand it. For example, think about, and even write down, new ideas and plans in your life. Sophie was a mother going back to work, but she felt lost and didn't have any idea what she wanted to do. This was reflected in her small 'mental' circle. To address this imbalance, she spent some time thinking about the jobs she wanted and made a list of them. She began to get excited at the prospects she was uncovering, her confidence grew and so did her mental circle – she was now up to the mental challenge of restarting her career.

Should your 'emotional' circle be the smallest, this shows you may have been hiding your innermost feelings. For example, maybe you are unhappy about some aspect of your relationship, but you haven't told your partner how you truly feel. Perhaps there's an ongoing argument in your family, but no-one is willing to discuss it. So how do you solve this? It is time to start talking about how you feel – using words like 'My feeling is . . .' – and to make a real effort to share your emotions more with close friends and family. You can also work on expanding your emotional circle by doing things that rouse your passions and feelings – watch a romantic movie or listen to a love song and lose yourself in the passion! Really begin to feel the emotions welling up inside you.

When your physical, mental and emotional circles are in balance be assured that your 'spiritual' circle will naturally and automatically expand as well. Even James, a die-hard engineer, had to admit his 'awareness of spirit' and 'other dimensions' had begun to blossom when his circles came into balance after he had completed The Wish!

Remember, this isn't a once-only exercise. You can draw your circles again at any time, and you'll be amazed how they will have changed. This exercise is especially helpful when you're feeling a little off balance, as it will always gives you a great snapshot of where you're at right now. You will find that adjusting your circles – by strengthening the areas where you are weak – will reflect both inwards and outwards in your life. You can do this exercise almost anywhere as well, as long as you have paper and a pen or pencil.

When your circles are all the same size, you'll know you're in balance – you will find all elements in your life are in natural harmony, and you will be energised, attract many friends and love will be radiating from you. Congratulations!

The exercises you have completed so far give you

real insight into who you really are and how your life is at this moment. More than this, they are helping you expand your energy field. As your power builds and increases, you will find that you are able to attempt and accomplish more, increasing your drive and impetus to bring your wishes into your life and get the most from them. And this isn't about some time in the distant future – take it from me, this will already be happening.

> As your power builds and increases, you will find that you are able to attempt and accomplish more, increasing your drive and impetus to bring your wishes into your life and get the most from them.

16

It's all in the mind

As we move towards making our wishes come true, we need to pay close attention to the power of thought, because without direction the mind leaves us all at sea without a paddle. If you stop to think about it, you can see how our thoughts and attitudes constantly impact us in so many ways.

Most people would have heard of the 'placebo effect'. Since publication of H.K. Beecher's *The Powerful Placebo* in 1955, studies have been done in the United States and elsewhere in which people were told they were being given medication but in fact the pills they took were nothing more than sugar. Despite this, the recipients stated that the medication improved their health – they *thought* they were receiving helpful medication and this mentally triggered a positive physical response. This revelation became known as the 'placebo effect'. These studies show that when we truly believe something is good for us, it becomes so. Indeed, a major study in 2008 found that SSRI antidepressant psychiatric drugs are no more effective than a placebo in treating depression.

Through many studies, we've now learned that the power of the mind can, and does, exert significant control over potential healing processes. When we *believe* in positive outcomes, our body is flooded with endorphins, chemicals which make us feel good and suppress pain. This means we can induce the release of endorphins, and MRI and PET scans show this is possible. What I take from this is that the mind can work powerfully for or against you, depending on whether you believe and accept what is being said or shown to you. So we all need to take care when it comes to those TV adverts on wrinkle cream! We regularly unconsciously absorb such information in our brains and the mind then automatically processes them for us, determining our course of action.

Similar studies have also identified what is known as the 'nocebo effect'. These studies looked at the links between negativity and poor health, and found that depression, severe grief, hopelessness and despair can plunge people into a downward spiral of unexpected health deterioration. So without doubt our thoughts can have the most powerful effect on our lives for good or bad.

What does this have to do with wishes manifesting? The power of your belief system creates your perception. What you believe in is what you draw to you – and your thoughts hold the power to make it happen. For example, recently I realised I had double-booked myself with two appointments at the same time. I gave thought to the one that I wished to cancel and saw it happening, and smiled. The next day I received a call from that person apologising for having to cancel their appointment! So be assured, strong thoughts – positive or negative – can and do dramatically impact your life.

What you believe in is what you draw to you – and your thoughts hold the power to make it happen.

One of the most perceptive researchers into the power of suggestion, Stuart Wolf, in 'The pharmacology of placebos' (*Journal of Clinical Investigation*, 1950), said, 'Mind mechanisms of the body are capable of reacting not only to direct physical and chemical stimulation, but also to symbolic stimuli, words and events which have somehow acquired special meaning for the individual.' Similarly, Dr Brian Olshansky, a professor of medicine at the University of Iowa, stated in a *Times* article called 'Thinking yourself sick' (25 August 2007) that a doctor's bedside manner is critical, as 'a cold, uncaring doctor will encourage a nocebo effect'.

Because we are all highly affected by the power of thought, it is important for your mind to be fully controlled by you, *for you*. It's the only way you can successfully process information that tells you whether something is good, bad or seriously damaging for you. Taking charge of your thoughts on a daily basis will enrich and nourish you and make it so much easier for your wishes to come true. Remember, the force within you must be ignited in order to create your wish. The energy itself has to be built up positively and enhanced with strong, determined thought and then unleashed by using your conscious mind to direct your thoughts constructively – this is the ultimate creation of The Wish.

Taking charge of your thoughts on a daily basis will enrich and nourish you and make it so much easier for your wishes to come true.

17

Get to the heart of things

You are now going to get to the heart of the matter. By now you should have a much greater sense of who you really are, and as you contemplate your wishlist, you will have reached a crucial point and may be asking the following questions: how do I know whether what I wish for is right for me? How can I be sure my wish will make a real difference to my life? How do I know it won't end up delivering more of the same, or even making my life worse?

These are really important questions. We must all take great care about what we wish for. The good news is that when we're meticulous and precise about what we desire, miracles happen. Sometimes, though, our wishes may not be exactly what we expected. Karen, who works in the entertainment industry in Los Angeles, told me her wish had been for the ideal man to come into her life. Within two weeks Hans arrived on the scene; he was perfect and Karen was ecstatic. Yet six months later the relationship was over, and Karen couldn't understand what had gone wrong and why her wish hadn't worked.

Well, of course it worked – exactly as she had created it. Karen wished for the ideal man and it was indeed the perfect time for the exact relationship that she had 'called in' – but for a limited period of time, not for life! I explained to Karen that she had outgrown the relationship at the end of that time and was therefore ready for something – or someone – much more suited to her newfound progress. Some of us get so caught up in imagining that everything we create will cover the rest of our lives, we forget that sometimes our need is for 'now' and not 'forever'.

So how do we know what's for our highest good?

This is where your wish-making gets really exciting. I'm now going to take you on the most sensational part of your journey – understanding your heart/soul connection, which then leads to the all-important 'Soul Test'. Once learned, this simple yet powerful technique will give you the ability to ask *any* question you want answered, drawing on your soul's own innate wisdom and truth. This test will not fail you, I promise. And the best thing about it is that you can use it anytime and anywhere.

Let's get started. First, it's all a matter of listening to your heart. This is not just another cliché, it's a fact. Why? Because we are nothing without our hearts. Our hearts don't just influence our lives physically, they have a huge impact on us emotionally, mentally, spiritually. It's strange that even though our heart is the most vital part of us, we tend to take it for granted. We expect it to carry on working for us regardless of whatever else is going on in our lives.

Our hearts don't just influence our lives physically, they have a huge impact on us emotionally, mentally, spiritually.

Yet every day our hearts offer us all kinds of amazing gifts. They bring that elusive 'x-factor' to everything we do. When we put all of our hearts into our relationships, our work and our ideas, success follows. We're able to take others with us, to attract new people and opportunities, to feel energised, satisfied, complete. When we begin to operate at our heart level, we have the very real sensation of awakening within. It's like looking around you and seeing the world for the first time. Nothing seems ordinary or unimportant any more. Imagine being able to experience life like this all the time. Can you feel your heart beating a little faster at the very thought of it? If it's not beating faster now, it soon will be.

> **When we begin to operate at our heart level, we have the very real sensation of awakening within.**

The way we refer to the heart in our everyday life gives us lots of clues about just how much it matters. For example, when we talk about the importance of something, we want to 'get to the heart of the matter'. And, once there, we have the deep joy of 'heart-to-heart' talks, where we truly experience our 'heartfelt' feelings. And how often do our hearts 'skip a beat' when we're shocked, or 'flutter' when we're excited, nervous or unsure? It happens to each and every one of us, and never more so than when we are experiencing the deepest and most telling 'affairs of the heart'.

The heart has also been identified with truth from time immemorial. For the ancient Egyptians, how someone fared in the afterlife depended on the weighing of their heart against the feather of Ma'at (Truth). The Egyptians believed the real person was defined by what lay in their heart. Even today, when you say something with your 'hand on heart' or use the words 'cross my heart and hope to die', you are expecting others to believe that what you are telling them is straight from your heart, so they cannot doubt you.

So if you really want to know what your purpose is in life, and why your soul has chosen for you to be here at this time, you will need to listen closely to your heart. While you may find it hard at first to make this connection, once made your ability to connect with your soul through your heart will remain throughout your life and, with practice, will only get stronger over time.

We've all had glimpses of this clarity, an 'inner knowing' that tells us we're making the right decision, going in the right direction – you have your heart to thank for this. I remember one occasion when my heart told me I shouldn't take the trip to Paris on a particular day. Thank goodness I listened. The train broke down and the passengers were stranded for many hours.

There's a deeper aspect to the heart which is rather special. We all have a soul, and our soul is joined to our physical body during earthly life. And I believe that your soul is attached to your body through the very centre of your heart. I choose to call this spot the 'soul's entrance'. Not surprisingly, it is also the soul's exit route on death.

This is critical, I believe, because our heart/soul connection is the most essential part, the core, of who we are. Interestingly, during the earliest days of heart surgery, I understand that surgeons realised there was an area they had to avoid when operating: it seems that if they touched this particular spot the patient would die. I believe this has enormous significance as it is the same spot where the soul holds its attachment to the physical part of us. Our heart is literally connected to our soul and if the connection is accidentally severed, it can result in our physical death. Put another way, this is the hotspot where the deep wisdom and insight of the soul meets the body – which is why we must listen to our hearts.

The difficulty for many of us is that we live almost continually in our heads and so we don't listen to what our hearts are trying to tell us. Hearts basically don't get a look-in. Don't worry. The process we'll look at shortly involves reinstating the 'live' connection between your true self and your soul, and you do this through your heart.

While this connection – and the Soul Test which reinstates it – will at first seem magical, it's actually a very practical method for seeking and receiving direct divine guidance. The answers you get will always be the most honest and truthful, as they are yours, and they can cover absolutely anything and everything you wish or need to know in your life. This is because your soul already holds all the answers for your highest and greatest good.

So, how does this work?

Instead of relying on others to provide all you wish for, which is patently unfair and impossible, you learn to trust in yourself first and foremost – in all that you think or do. You will also learn not to expect too much of anyone else. This is genuine empowerment. Think about it. When you put your trust in someone – be it a family member, close friend, partner, lover, acquaintance or work colleague – you will find that somehow, at some time, they will appear to let you down and you will feel dreadfully disappointed as a result. However, you can't expect others to know exactly what you need all the time, because it is you who has the heart/soul connection.

Learning to understand and trust your heart/soul connection is a fundamental part of your journey through life. And it's a lesson that gets repeated again and again until you discover how to connect with your soul and hold a greater 'knowing' of yourself and, in turn, others. You achieve this by learning to stay within your own field of empowerment.

Then it will become second nature for you to take charge and trust yourself – to live as the true 'you'. Once you understand, acknowledge and begin to live in this way, your energy field will begin to expand and you will become more intuitive, more 'in tune' with your inner knowing. Then you will hold in your hands yet another golden key towards personal fulfilment.

You may already have heard of the saying, 'The body never lies.' Well, this is true, but only when you have open communication with your soul through your physical body. Once you are able to do this, then you have the key to the Kingdom of Life itself – you can access everything you are ready for or want to know.

Let me explain in a little more detail how we access the heart/soul connection. The reason I speak so often about relaxation, taking breaths and closing your eyes is because while we work our magic it is necessary to keep the physical body quiet, which of course includes resting the 'toolbox'. Only then can your conscious mind send commands to your soul via your heart centre without any interruptions. This also allows us to naturally slip into a perfect state where our brain waves are on a line between alpha and theta, a level I call 'Code A' (as covered in more detail in my first book, *The Secrets of Psychic Success*).

Code A is actually the brain frequency that matches the earth's frequency – about 7.83 hertz per second – and all life forms on earth exist on this frequency. However, for humanity, over the last hundred years or so, life has sped up and advanced at such a rate, and continues to get ever faster, that we all start mentally screaming and buzzing inside our heads, wincing from the increasing pressures of our lives, and suffering more and more stress symptoms. It seems to me now that most people spend their thinking time on a much higher, speedier frequency, one frenziedly dominated by texts, tweets, emails, apps and all manner of instant communications which have them rushing around, leaving them without any time to be calm and serene, let alone find Code A – which is the frequency you must be on if you are to succeed with the Soul Test and your wish-making.

First, you must do some preliminary connecting with your soul. Here's a simple relaxation process to create that sense of calm within you.

Begin by finding somewhere quiet where you can sit on a comfortable chair or sofa; some of you may find it easier to lie down on the floor or even on a bed. Make sure you will not be disturbed – that means no phones!

Now, for a few moments, close your eyes. Put your hands in your lap. Take a breath in and let it go; do this three times. Remind yourself to let your shoulders drop back and relax. Think of something that makes you happy – an experience you have enjoyed or would like to enjoy, like walking in the park with someone you love, or relaxing on that perfect beach.

When you have this experience clearly in your mind, say these words to yourself: 'I am now calm

Get to the heart of things

and deeply relaxed.' Take another breath in and let it go while telling yourself, 'I am now becoming more and more deeply relaxed.' With your eyes closed, for a moment focus all your thought on your right hand (or your left hand, if you're left-handed) and imagine a feeling of touch in your fingers. Really feel the sensation. Then take a breath in and let it go. Place this hand on your heart.

Put your other hand on top of the hand already on your heart. Do not cross your hands, just place them one on top of the other on your heart region. Stay relaxed and focus your thought on the hand that is touching your heart. Concentrate and focus all of your thought-power into feeling the sensation of your heartbeat with your hand.

Say in your mind, 'I am now feeling my heart-beat.' When you start feeling the sensation of your heart beating beneath your palm and fingers, you are now in touch with your soul. Congratulations! Take a breath, let it go, smile – you can open your eyes.

The Wish

In this simple little process you have begun your amazing journey to connect with the wiser, greater, truer part of yourself. At the moment we're simply using this exercise to relax. You can even do this before going to sleep, as this is a time when you are naturally more at ease. As you'll soon see, there's a lot more we can do once we understand the heart/soul connection. It's exciting because now you've started to gain greater awareness and empowerment, and you'll soon be living your life exactly as you wish.

18

Intention is everything

Your intention, my intention, a friend's intention – what is it? I remember my grandmother saying things like 'He had such good intentions, he wasn't to know it was going to backfire.' Whatever our intentions, they can still go astray, unless of course we have a complete understanding of how to work with them towards a positive outcome. This is more easily achieved when you are calm, prepared and organised, and ready to direct the thought-command fluidly through to its desired conclusion. As the saying goes, 'It is not the deed but the thought behind the deed.'

I remember one occasion when I was sitting at my desk. Even though I was working, I was quite relaxed.

The Wish

I thought about a close girlfriend, and in my mind I saw her laughing and chatting with me about a trip we were going to take together to India, and I smiled to myself. It was a fleeting moment, but it was focused, purely utilising thought-intention. Within minutes the phone rang and it was my girlfriend, saying, 'Now, about this trip to India . . .'

Another time the lease was up at the house where my husband Andrew and I were living and we had less than two months to find a new home. We have dogs, and it is more difficult to find a place that accepts animals. Through my thought-intention I had visualised the perfect home but I hadn't put any restrictions on where it should be, I just added 'in the most divine way'. While we were giving thought to a new home, Andrew and I had to attend a wedding so I asked a close friend, Beverley, if she would dog-sit for the day. She agreed, and added, 'What else would you like me to do while you're away? Otherwise I'll get bored.' So I told her we were looking for somewhere to live, just a small place, but would love a garden for the dogs, and left her to it. Andrew and I arrived home from the wedding quite late. Beverley greeted us and said, 'I've had a great day. I went through the newspapers and I've made you an appointment to see a place in two days' time. It's absolutely right for you.' The place she found was ideal for us and had a great garden for our dogs. We moved in a month later.

This may seem almost too simple, but often the great truths are so simple they're overlooked. By reading these words you are already increasing your awareness and understanding, and giving greater thought to your life experiences. You are using the process of thought expansion. To practise focusing your intention on what you truly want in your life, first you must start living 'in the now', not living for tomorrow, and most certainly not for yesterday. Time is purely a man-made concept that evolved to help us plan, understand where we're at and survive, but it's not all there is. You need to start thinking in terms of living as if each day is the first day of your life. This is the only way you can then conceive a plan for all you wish for.

To practise focusing your intention on what you truly want in your life, first you must start living 'in the now', not living for tomorrow, and most certainly not for yesterday.

So far we have looked at the importance of making a command and then directing the power of your thought-intention into your hand to feel your heart, so you activate your heart/soul connection. But the power of your thought-intention can be directed in more exciting ways to help with everyday issues as well.

During my courses I regularly have to remind people to breathe when they're doing the thought-intention exercises – they can get so tied up in their thoughts and intentions, it's easy to forget to breathe! We always have a laugh about it, which is an incredibly beneficial way of reducing any tension and bringing about even greater self-healing and further relax-ation. Once you've defined your intention a few times, you will find it gets much easier to make and give commands to yourself. Trust in your own evidence as everything starts slipping divinely into place.

The crucial point is for you to recognise that you have the power to direct your thought for positive intention, whether to benefit your health, to build your self-love, or to create the perfect outcome for that date, appointment or meeting, or whatever you need to do. Everything can be changed by thought and positive intention. How you feel, what you do, who you wish to be, who you wish to meet next – all is made possible when you give yourself that moment to plan your thoughts and direct them positively.

> **Everything can be changed by thought and positive intention.**

For example, say you would love a kitten or even a new car for your birthday: create it in picture form and go on to see yourself receiving it as a gift. Or, should you have a pain somewhere, you can visualise that pain and give it a colour to associate it with: if it is very bad, maybe you'll see it as red, which is the colour that holds the strongest and most active wave-form. Now see it cleared and surrounded in healing white light – you'll find the red disappears when you use a thought-command to restore everything to perfect working order. This is a great technique I use myself and recommend to clients and friends.

To give you an even clearer picture of how important it is for you to have strength of intention, I want to share with you the following experiment undertaken by the Institute of HeartMath in the 1990s. It's all about thought-intention and blood cells. Samples of white blood cells were taken from donors and the donors were put in one room while their individual blood cells were put in suitable measuring chambers inside another room in the same building, where any electrical changes in them could be carefully monitored. The donors were then subjected to emotional stimulation using video clips, varied in content and therefore generating very different reactions. When the donors showed highs and lows of emotional reaction, measured electrically, their blood cells exhibited identical responses at exactly the same moments – the peaks and troughs on the graphs of the blood cells instantly matched those of the donors.

The tests continued, with the cells left where they were and the donors moved up a floor; then into the building next door; then into the next block; then a mile away. What the experimenters found – and confirmed with repeated tests – was that even with a distance of 50 miles between the cells and the donors, it made no difference at all: the responses between the donors and their cells were still instant and identical.

So when you are ready to use your intention to make something happen, first give yourself time for careful thought, planning all you want to achieve. The power is within you to do so, to direct your thought positively, as the evidence in scientific tests now shows.

19

The Soul Test

I had come to a point where I wanted to change my career and I needed to know if I was going in the right direction. I did the Soul Test and it was very revealing. The answers were not what I expected at all. Even though it wasn't what I thought I wanted, I decided to listen to what my soul was telling me – and now I'm very happy in my new job.

– **Susan, industrial designer, Sydney and London**

I use the Soul Test often – it really does give you a direction to take positive action and do something, rather than just sit and wait for a result.

– **Jenny, human resources manager, London**

The Soul Test

Now you have your heart/soul connection and the know-how to use the power of intention, you are absolutely ready for the 'Soul Test'. I believe the Soul Test is the most dynamic breakthrough you can or will ever make. Once you realise its incredible potential towards personal freedom and empowerment, it will give you the opportunity to get the most benefit from your life from now on.

The Soul Test is unique. When I discovered it, it blew me away. When I fully appreciated and understood what it was that I was being shown, I was so excited I could hardly contain myself. So I put the technique through its paces, which meant working with as many people as I could to test it thoroughly in every way before going 'live'. And it worked, and still does.

The Soul Test goes to the very heart of choosing what's right for you in this lifetime. It can be used at any time and anywhere – a simple, straightforward but extraordinarily telling technique which will answer any and every question you have.

The Soul Test goes to the very heart of choosing what's right for you in this lifetime.

Once you start using the Soul Test, you'll find it's something you will use more and more as time goes on, because it will never let you down. Best of all, it will steer you towards your highest good. This is what makes it such a critical life tool, especially at this time when increasingly so many are feeling lost and helpless amid growing global uncertainty, where individual values and people's identities are progressively being eroded and diminished. Unfortunately, this has become very much part of our modern society with an ever-hungry media regularly telling us that there's war here or there, that people are starving, that our children are obese, that unemployment is on the increase, that the financial markets are falling. Not to mention the advertising campaigns which tell us that we can only look and feel good if we buy this or that product.

That's why belief in yourself, your identity, and

knowing your true role here on Earth is absolutely vital for your personal fulfilment. And the Soul Test helps make this possible.

Jim was a director of a successful international interior design company. For all the supposed glamour of his position, he was seriously unhappy with his business situation. He felt trapped by his business partner, a bullying control freak who wouldn't listen to anyone else's ideas or creative suggestions, let alone agree with Jim on how best to promote and develop their company internationally. So the one burning problem Jim felt he had was how to make real decisions, ones that could bring about positive change.

Through The Wish Jim gained immense inner strength, recognising and confronting his worries and fears. He succeeded in making a decision towards realising the 'planned creation' of his own future, and then tested it with the Soul Test and found it positive. Five months later Jim was amazingly happy. His whole persona had altered. He had left the old company, having been profitably bought out, and had set up his own design business with some really talented people.

Now you have read what the Soul Test can do for others, let's try it out.

First, think about what it is you ache to know. It could be something quite simple to start with, like finding out if you should go on that date, attend that party, buy that second-hand car or go for that job interview. The best thing about communicating directly with your soul is that it helps you separate what you *think* you want from what you *truly* want – that is, what will really enhance and fulfil you and is therefore absolutely right for you. So when doing the Soul Test, always use the words 'For my highest and greatest good' at the beginning of any statement. This ensures that you get what is the best for you. It also saves you wasting all that time, energy and, in some cases, possibly a good part of your life being somewhere that isn't advancing you. If you leave these words out, you're effectively settling for second best.

The Soul Test

Once you know what you want to check, you can put together a statement for your soul to respond to. Keep your words simple and always speak 'in the now'. Be direct and clear. You can write down your statement if you prefer, to make sure it's exactly as you want it.

Let's say you want to know if you should or should not take a job with a company called 'Fairban'. Then your statement would be: 'For my highest and greatest good I am now working for Fairban.' Note the use of the present tense bringing your statement into the now: it's vital that anything you wish to know is always spoken of as occurring in the present – in the now.

Then, if you want to check how long you will work there, you can state, 'For my highest and greatest good I am working for Fairban for up to six months.' You can check a shorter or longer timeframe, it's up to you. Often a job is really good for us in the short term but not forever. Ultimately, time as we see it is an illusion. All possibilities reside in the now.

Whenever you do this, you must say your

statement three times. The first time it will not fully register, the second time it is taken onboard, and the third time gives your statement the certainty it needs for your heart/soul connection to respond.

Now you're ready to try the Soul Test for yourself. Stand up with your feet together. If you're inside, stand in the middle of the room without any furniture or objects too close by, as your body can move and topple forwards, backwards or even sideways depending on the soul's response.

Feel the excitement welling up within you – but be calm in your body. Take a breath in and let it go. Remind yourself of the words you are going to use and then close your eyes.

Put your left hand over your right hand (vice versa if you are left-handed) over the heart region. Always put the statement to your soul while your hands are placed on your heart region, because you're now fully activating and using the heart/soul connection that you learned about earlier. Repeat the statement three times. When you say it the third time, you will notice that your body will move in one direction, rather like a pendulum.

This is how it works:

If your body starts to fall forward, it means 'yes' to your statement; that is, your soul supports your wish. For some people it can be quite a strong forward movement, but regardless of how strong the movement is, as long as you feel the pull is forward you know your soul has given its stamp of approval. This means that what you wish for is positive and for your highest good.

If your soul does not support what you desire, then your body will pull or topple backwards. Again, for some people this can be quite a strong backwards movement. While this may not be the answer you were looking for, at least now you know not to waste time and energy on this particular endeavour: it will not be, so let it go and move on to something that better enhances your life!

If your body starts wobbling from side to side, it means there's confusion. So it's not a 'no', nor is it a 'yes'. Sometimes the way you frame the statement has not allowed for all the potential options that exist about what you wanted to know. For instance, if you want to find out if you are going to Sabina's party with Gary on a set date, your statement should be: 'For my highest and greatest good I am at Sabina's party with Gary on 28 May.' If you were any less specific as to Gary, the date and the event, then the wobble would be telling you either you are going to the party but not with Gary, or you are going to be with Gary on that date but not going to the party! So you'll need to rephrase your statement to be sure.

If your body goes sideways, you need to give more thought to your statement and be very clear about what it is that you want, and then reword your statement to suit. Don't worry, though: when you get a little more used to the Soul Test technique, it will become second nature! The secret is to always keep it simple.

What does it mean when you have made your statement and your body doesn't move at all? There are times when you get no movement in your body, and actually your soul is responding in truth to you because you weren't really bothered either way. Or maybe you just weren't taking it seriously enough!

Let's try some other questions so you can get the hang of the Soul Test.

For example, you may want to know if your new relationship is the one for you, so you would say, '**For my highest and greatest good (his/her name) is the perfect one for me at this time.**'

Or you could say, '**For my highest and greatest good I am married to (his/her name) on (date).**'

Or even, '**For my highest and greatest good I am having a relationship with (his/her name) for up to ten months.**' (Or whatever period you choose.)

How about a dream holiday, somewhere exotic you have always wanted to visit – let's say you want to go to Singapore. You would frame your statement in this way: '**For my highest and greatest good I am visiting Singapore within twelve months.**' If you get a 'yes' (i.e. your body moved forwards) you can narrow the time down to fewer months or even suggest an actual month in the year, e.g. '**For my highest and greatest good I am visit-**

ing Singapore in March this year.' Or you could actually specify a year and say, **'For my highest and greatest good I am visiting Singapore in March 2014.'**

Sheryl was worried when she did her first Soul Test. She had just joined a new company which she loved and when she did her statement – 'For my highest and greatest good I am working for X' – she fell backwards. Because Sheryl had not specified how long she was working with this company, the answer was 'no' – she wasn't to be working for this company for the rest of her life! Sheryl then reworded the statement to be more specific: 'For my highest and greatest good I am working with X for up to twelve months.' She fell forwards and was delighted as well as relieved. (As it turned out, before the twelve months were up she went on to another job that was even better!)

Emma is an American living in Brussels. Being the head of production for a successful US film company, her work takes her all over the world. She is continually travelling to the major cities in Europe as well as back and forth to the States. She lives her career 24/7, and when I first met her I realised she never gave time to herself or even her dearly loved little dog. Emma had been in several relationships that had come and gone in quick succession and she wanted to know if she would ever meet the man of her dreams and have a lifelong relationship.

Taking the Soul Test revealed many truths. While there was no doubt Emma was very good at her job, she felt her whole life was quickly passing her by. By focusing on the relationship she wanted, instead of giving all of her time and energy to her work, Emma discovered what was waiting for her – which was a new, real and loving relationship with 'the one'. The Soul Test even told her when they would meet – and they did! Her only problem now is making time for the two of them to enjoy and build on their precious relationship.

Once you've learned how to work with the Soul Test, it will always be there for you as you need it. You can now ask your soul any question at any time, anywhere, on anything you truly wish to know. When you have this hotline to your soul, there is no need for any more procrastination or doubt. Through this simple technique, you will gain so much more energy because all that wasted, needless worry and concern has been removed. Now you can go on to become a fully self-assured, charismatic individual, continually increasing your field of energy towards self-empowerment and true 'knowing'.

> When you have this hotline to your soul, there is no need for any more procrastination or doubt.

20

The tides of synchronicity

The Wish is your biggest wake-up call, offering some of the most exceptional insights for living. It is a gift to you. You'll begin noticing the difference as each day brings synchronicities. Synchronicity is usually found in everyday life on an infrequent and very much hit-and-miss basis; now, though, you are successfully able to join all the dots through increased awareness as you are filled with positive energy. This is a moment when you can feel an inner warmth and enjoy that feeling of love within – and send out thoughts of gratitude for every opportunity that comes your way.

One of the secrets of The Wish is to recognise the incredible power of synchronicity, as it takes on a life and energy of its own. When you know yourself and feel fully empowered to positively benefit your daily life and enjoy living in the moment, something quite amazing opens up before you.

You will find all this empowerment brings a tremendously exciting sense of inner knowing. You feel – and are – balanced, energised and in the flow. You get up in the morning and your personal frequency already starts emitting positive signals. This is your shining light, as each thought you energise starts performing by way of occurrences starting to take place – such as when you're thinking about your mother or sister, and the next minute they call you. Or maybe you're on holidays and suddenly remember you've got to buy a birthday card and walk around the corner to see a card shop. Perhaps you're having a coffee with friends and start chatting about an old boyfriend you haven't seen for years, and the next minute he walks in.

One of the most delightful examples was a friend of mine who had just received a huge electricity bill and had no way of paying it. She put out the thought for assistance and felt that something good would happen. Two days later she received a tax refund cheque in the post – and for the exact amount of the electricity bill, too!

> **When you know yourself and feel fully empowered to positively benefit your daily life and enjoy living in the moment, something quite amazing opens up before you.**

Nathan, a lawyer, had just moved apartments in New York. When he unpacked his things in his new place, he realised he had lost his favourite book. He looked everywhere, but it was nowhere to be found and he was very upset. A few days later Nathan had to attend a meeting in another part of the city, and on the way there he felt pulled to walk into a nearby market. As he went in, he noticed a second-hand book stall. He went over to the stall, and to his great delight he saw a copy of his favourite book. He picked it up and opened it, and to his utter amazement he saw his name on the inside cover – it was his lost book.

Only last week I was speaking to a new client on the phone and I asked her how she had found me. She replied, in a very matter-of-fact way, 'I was in a bookshop and a book suddenly fell off one of the shelves and onto the floor – your face on the front cover was looking up at me. So I decided to Google you and make contact.'

Here's an example of synchronicity from my own life. Andrew and I have made many trips to India to have readings with the Naadis in Delhi, about which we wrote in our book, *The Hidden Oracle of India*. On every trip there have been nine of us. Last year, though, there were only eight of us booked to go on the trip, and while we were at the airport waiting for our flight, I quietly wondered why this was. 'All very strange,' I thought. Andrew went to get a cup of coffee, and when he came back he said excitedly, 'You'll never guess who I've just seen!' It turned out to be Simon, a very good friend of ours who we hadn't seen in months, who happened to be travelling to India for business on the same plane. When Andrew explained why we were going to India, Simon asked if he could join us, as he had always wanted to meet the Naadis. He did – and our group was nine again!

All these examples show how we can connect to the power of synchronicity. Through focusing on exciting new ideas and thought-full plans, you will open your mind to the greater and bigger picture. In turn you will calmly become the full and completely competent being you truly are, and an inner glow of satisfaction will expand within you. Synchronicities will become commonplace along your beautiful new pathway to life. Better still, as you progress, the miracle moments will become more frequent.

You will calmly become the full and completely competent being you truly are, and an inner glow of satisfaction will expand within you.

The Wish

As you work with The Wish insights, you'll see for yourself that now it is you who is in charge of your life. *You* are the maker of your own destiny. Living life to your full potential will make your days more harmonious and energising. Everything will take on a new meaning and manifest itself in the right time and the right way.

21

The golden light to self-healing

As we've seen, you can create anything you want for your highest good through the power of your directed thoughts. Amazingly, though, you can also learn to heal yourself in an extraordinary and miraculous way. Whether you're suffering pain, a cold, a rash, a headache or an even more serious condition, this method is something you can add to your medicine cabinet, ready for times when you feel under the weather. It's important to stress that I am not, for one moment, saying that you shouldn't consult your doctor when the need arises, but I recommend you read on to see just what you can do for yourself.

Self-healing is all about taking back the initiative

and becoming responsible for your own health. This technique uses thought-commands to alter your body patterns so that they change back into 'healthy mode'. You have got it in you to do this, and it is all linked to your newfound ability.

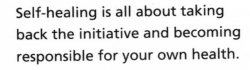

Self-healing is all about taking back the initiative and becoming responsible for your own health.

I wrote earlier of DNA and the power of visualisation in healing our DNA. This method of self-healing is accomplished by working your commands with a similar visualisation technique and coupling it with a deep sense of feeling in your body. Yes, it's that simple, yet it is an immensely powerful method that I have personally used many times whenever I've needed it, and for me it has always worked with amazing immediacy. This is because I believe anything is possible and that our thought-commands achieve whatever we wish them to.

The following technique allows you the opportunity

to give your belief system time to embrace the miracle that can and does take place.

Whenever the need arises, lie flat on the floor somewhere quiet. Close your eyes, relax and take a few breaths in and out. Tell yourself, 'I am now deeply relaxed.' Repeat this three times, without haste.

Focus your thought on the specific area of your body that requires healing. Now add your command in words for the illness to leave you, as with the following example.

These are the three vital components:

First, visualise the zone or area in your body where the pain, rash, lump or whatever is. Then see that area being healed – and hold the image – until the area is seen by you to be fully healed and looking healthy again. At the same time use these words of command, speaking to yourself in the second person: 'You are now functioning in perfect health, fully energised in harmony and balance.'

This is a thought-command, so your body knows that it is happening right now.

Second, give the same command, adding two specific dates in the future (say, a date one month and three months ahead), and see them one after the other, with your body perfectly healed on each date. For example, 'On 1 March you are now functioning in perfect health, fully energised in harmony and balance.'

Finally, use your emotions and actually feel the sensation of perfect health inside you – feel the love inside, and the joy. Take a few breaths in and out, and feel the difference.

Remember, too, the experiment with white blood cells and what those donors accomplished without realising it. You can change your body cells every bit as instantly and as effectively as they did, even when they were miles apart at the time. Your thought-intention can have just as powerful an effect on your physical body as it does on your mental, spiritual and emotional wishes.

22

Develop your sense of knowing

We have all heard people talk about having a 'gut instinct' or a 'hunch'. Some of us may say things like, 'I don't know how I know, I just know.' Or maybe you've had a 'feeling' that something was wrong, or you knew 'deep down inside'. But what does it all actually mean?

These are all instinctive responses – similar to a fight or flight reaction to a threat or danger – which come from our solar plexus, causing a sense of either excitement or foreboding within us. When you act on your instinct, it will benefit you. This is because when you listen to your gut instinct, or you have a hunch, you are fully and completely trusting in your 'self', your inner knowing. And the more you listen to your sense of knowing, the more it will give you the necessary boost to follow through on your instincts.

Your instinct is an unquestionably powerful force in helping you make the right choices in all you do and say, and in all that takes place around you from this moment on. With all the Wish insights you will soon have a wonderful 'sense of knowing' coming into play. This happens when you become fully aware of yourself and the world around you: there will be stronger internal signals that you will very quickly learn to act upon.

Here's an example that's all too common. Some years back my twin sister Engie was booking a holiday with a friend and they had to choose between two dates for their flight. She felt a terrible sense of foreboding about the first date – and I must add I supported her on this. So they chose the second date, exactly a week later, and booked their flight. On the first date, the plane crashed and everyone onboard was killed.

On another occasion I was handed a magazine and, while flipping through it, I noticed something that I don't normally spend a second on – a competition. Only this time my eye was drawn to keep looking at it, and at the same time there was this powerful sense of 'knowing' that I would win it. So I completed the form and sent it in straightaway, then promptly forgot all about it. Three months later I was contacted with a great big 'congratulations' letter – I'd won!

So never dismiss this incredibly powerful and beneficial heart/soul connection that now feeds and nourishes your life. It allows you to know a whole lot more than you did previously when you were shut down by your fears, stress and exhaustion. You'll find this new ability to read people and situations as they really are is a very valuable life skill.

Never dismiss this incredibly powerful and beneficial heart/soul connection that now feeds and nourishes your life.

It's not just overall feelings and impressions that will get a boost: your heart/soul connection will sharpen and enliven your five physical senses as well. You'll find you develop a more acute sense of vision, hearing, touch, smell and taste – it will enhance all that you do as you expand your complete awareness to life, to friends, family and all that is going on around you.

So let's look at what a 'sense of knowing' means. In one way it's rather like becoming a tuning fork; as you cause these alterations to take place, so you become more 'sensitive' and in tune with your surroundings and with the rest of life as well.

Even more amazing is your sixth sense. Your intuition will naturally activate and offer you the ability to 'see' in your mind's eye – that is, momentary inner-vision. Someone might be talking to you about their sick father and you suddenly get an image of him or maybe you can feel his pain in you. You find yourself 'picking up' his energy. This gives you evidence of your increasing powers, and can become a lifelong aid that can greatly assist all those around you, and – if you so wished – allow you to be of service to others in a divinely beneficial way. All in all, your sixth sense will only improve as you progress to complete The

Wish. It may seem too subtle at first but with continual use, belief and nurture, it too will become second nature to you.

Each step is a wake-up call to your consciousness, impacting your ability to read situations, recognise what's good for you and in so doing expand your powers. A nice bonus will be a heightened appreciation of the natural world as well. So whatever you do in nature, from an afternoon in the garden to a walk in the local park or a hike in the mountains, will be much more enjoyable as you immerse yourself in the sheer sensuality of the experience as well as savouring the huge positive impact nature so generously gives out through its continual powerful energy when felt and absorbed.

From now on your soul will keep you in close touch with your feelings and radiate love from your heart. You'll start noticing that friends and strangers sense your warmth and are drawn towards you. And with your heightened emotions, you will be able to know whether to trust them or not, from the sensations you get in your solar plexus, when your inner knowing comes into play for your benefit.

As you recognise these signals more and more, they will confirm to you your inner knowing about what you're doing, where you're going and whether you are around a person or in a situation that could be problematic. And when you act on your sense of knowing, you enhance your true potential a thousandfold.

All this is possible because your body responds to every single event that takes place. It's like a transmitter and receiver. So when you're able to recognise and understand the messages your body receives through your own intuitive 'sensing', it will be of immense benefit to you in the many decisions you have to make in your everyday life.

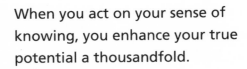

When you act on your sense of knowing, you enhance your true potential a thousandfold.

When you understand how much your inner knowing can help you regain control of your life by identifying the things that are genuinely good for you, then you are in a much better position to command anything and everything you desire. Add to this your ability with the Soul Test to then check whether what you want is absolutely right for you and for your highest and greatest good, and you will begin to see how truly empowering all of these resources are when they are used together.

23

Sharpen your memory

How often do you forget? We are especially likely to forget things when we are rushed and overly busy. It's easy these days to get bogged down with all the rushing around as well as all the texts, tweets, emails, etc., all demanding our attention. You get to the point where you can't think straight and so you easily forget the most important thing you needed to remember. Then you waste precious energy trying to remember or cover the cracks.

Earlier we looked at how all of your memories are held in your toolbox, the subconscious side of your brain. Because your toolbox becomes so crammed and jumbled, it becomes mentally very challenging trying to compute what you are looking for at just the right moment. Life becomes a muddle. We end up saying things like 'Just give me a moment, I can't think straight' or 'What was it that I needed to remember?'

Then there are those awful moments when you are attending a wedding and an acquaintance walks up and you are expected to introduce them to others around you, but you just can't remember their name! Or when it suddenly dawns on you that you've forgotten your wedding anniversary, or the password on your computer, or the vital piece of information you needed for an exam.

If you suffer from these memory lapses like many of us do, you can train yourself to remember, and you can do this through the power of your mind. As soon as you hear or see something that you mustn't forget, stop for a moment and use this technique.

Put your fingers and thumbs together, at stomach level, spread apart in front of you, pointing away from your stomach. Then say three times, in your mind or out loud, what it is you want to remember, take a breath in, and let the breath out as you release your hands. Now you're done.

If it's a birthday that you want to remember, for example, say the person's name and the date three times – for example, 'Marilyn's birthday, 12th March.' If it's a name that you have to remember – let's say it's John Benny – repeat 'John Benny' three times.

Later, as soon as you need to recall the name, birthday or whatever, just put your hands together in the same way, take a breath in and let it go. Within seconds your memory will give you whatever it is you want to remember.

Stuart tells me he uses this technique before any important sales meeting. He looks at the names of who is going to be present and goes through the steps, saying each of the names to himself three times. Then he walks into the meeting with great confidence, addressing each of the people by name. They are all so impressed! So far he has succeeded in using this method to remember up to ten names at a time.

This memory tip is especially fantastic when you

have a busy work schedule, but you can also use it to reinstate positive feelings and experiences. While you're doing The Wish, for example, you can use it to help hold the excitement and anticipation within you; simply use these words – **'I am now ready to create in my life'** – to recall your empowerment whenever you need to.

24

Awaken your power

As you will soon learn, to make a wish you need energy. Now, I know we all talk about having energy, yet few of us really think about what nourishes us beyond the food and exercise we think we need to build up the stamina to keep our physical bodies going. So when you lack energy is it because you are tired, or are you tired because you lack energy? And what sort of energy is it that you lack?

Daylight – sunlight – is the most vital source of energy for our minds and bodies, giving us our vitality as well as the greatest of feel-good factors. When you wake up in the morning and it is a beautiful day, the sun is shining and there is a clear blue sky, it naturally gives you an amazing energising boost. Daylight is an actual field of energy the sun emits, which increases throughout the day, and this increased energy field benefits our bodies. So even when the skies are grey and covered in cloud, we are still recharged as the field of vitality still fills the air and gets through to us.

This vitality promotes all forms of life on earth during daylight hours. There is a build-up of positive energy which is at its fullest by early evening, after which is the perfect time to recharge our depleted batteries. Then it slowly dissipates and is fully gone by midnight. This is why it's best to go to bed before midnight if you want to benefit from a full recharge. Another great way of recharging is to take a nap in the afternoon or early evening for half an hour while the energy field is at its fullest.

I have a friend who was always waking up in the early hours of the morning and couldn't get back to sleep – it was something that was really upsetting to her. I explained that the reason she couldn't go back to sleep once she'd woken up was because there was no energy left for her body to collect and so it couldn't beneficially recharge. She then realised that her way of life was so full-on, intense and speedy that she depleted her batteries and lost more energy than she could ever hope to put back. Now she has altered her sleep pattern and has a nap when she gets home from work, and, if she does wake up early in the morning, she doesn't fight it and instead gets up and does something she enjoys. If you have similar problems sleeping, try a new plan for your evenings and don't fret over it. It really does work.

We can also broaden the pool from which to recharge ourselves by tapping into cosmic energy, the energy that is always available to us from the universe. That's quite a concept to run with, I know, but easy to put into practice when you understand how. There are many books and websites that talk about this, so I won't go into much detail here. Briefly, though, each of us has three 'bodies' – our physical body, our 'etheric body' (sometimes known as the 'etheric double'), and our 'astral body'. While there are other energy zones within us, our etheric and astral bodies are the ones I want to talk about here.

The etheric body is a layer about three inches thick that surrounds and protects the physical body. It is a silvery, elasticated copy of your physical body. Your etheric body wraps around your physical one like a shield, and holds a record of any injuries, damage or trauma that you have incurred over the years, both internally and externally. This is what the great mystics can see and read. It is the powerhouse for the body: when you keep this etheric shield energised, your physical body has greater stamina and the ability to sail successfully through even the most stressful days.

The astral body is a ghostly traveller that slips out of the physical body for a short time – in most instances while we sleep – travelling around quite freely and gaining cosmic energy as it does so. Have you ever woken up with a start when you've fallen asleep on a train, bus or sofa? This is something that happens when we're tired and stressed, and basically it's when your astral body has slipped out of alignment with your physical body in order to gain as much cosmic energy as it can, quickly and urgently.

This suddenly causes us to jolt or have a sense of falling as our astral body shoots back into place and wakes us up.

There is another, more subtle field, too, that we cannot afford to ignore – this is commonly called the 'auric field' or aura. The auric field emits from the physical body, it gives off light energy and illustrates our current mental, physical, emotional and spiritual states – this is why we often hear sensitive people say things like, 'He has an amazing aura.'

One of the most important things to realise is that to be truly energised our three bodies – physical, etheric and astral – must be given the opportunity to stay fully and properly nourished. This allows us to remain in a balanced state, and gives us the exuberance that we need in our daily lives. So make sure you top up all your energy bodies. It will help you become a charismatic, fully empowered individual while successfully creating what you want in all areas of your life.

A friend who worked on stage in front of huge audiences knew very well that he had to build up his energy field before each performance. He always used the technique I am now going to give you: it works so well that he would come off stage at the end of every performance and still feel amazingly energised.

> **To be truly energised our three bodies – physical, etheric and astral – must be given the opportunity to stay fully and properly nourished.**

This is a speedy way for you to benefit from the immense energy reserves that exist at the many cosmically aligned ancient sites without you physically having to go there. It is done by using thought-command and can fill your etheric body with enough renewed energy to last for weeks. So, as tired as you may often be or feel, you can still take a few moments to totally replenish your energy reserves at any time. Most of us are aware of Stonehenge, so we will use this site as the energy booster.

The Wish

First, find somewhere quiet. Again, no phones! You will only need about five minutes to do this exercise. Stand up, take a breath in, let it go and close your eyes. Now in your mind create in front of you a cinema-sized screen with a bright blue frame. Put on the screen an image of the huge stones of Stonehenge standing upright on the grass. Now see your etheric body step out in front of you, facing the screen.

There is a lightning storm all around you on the screen – this helps you direct your thought to the centre of the stones. Using a strong thought-command, send a tube from the middle of the stones directly to your solar plexus, below the chest, in your etheric body. Then see it filling you with boundless energy, rather like filling your car with petrol. Watch as the energy pumps in. The moment you feel totally full, close off the pipeline and put your etheric body back into your physical body. Then close down the screen. Take a breath in, let it go, and smile. Open your eyes. You have just given yourself a big energy boost, one that can last for some time.

So how does that feel? You will find it makes you feel relaxed and completely calm. You can do this exercise regularly, such as once a week, or whenever you feel the need. It is also a wonderful way to boost your energy before you create your wish.

25

Build your strengths

We've done a lot of great work already on creating a much more dynamic you, so that you have sufficient positive power to make things happen in your life. Now you are going to build your strengths by creating your very own 'ring of confidence'. Your ring of confidence is a strong, powerful life force energy that surrounds you and acts as your own personal protection against any negative influences or events – for example, when someone loses it at the office, or your mother-in-law shouts at you, or someone gets angry in a traffic jam, or you're in a pub and a fight suddenly breaks out.

By using your newly enforced power of thought

you can create the most amazing 'ring of confidence' around you. This is such a simple little exercise, but it's so powerful.

First, think of something that makes you feel happy, say an experience that you've really enjoyed, like time spent with a friend when something very funny happened and made you laugh till you ached. Once you have that stimulating thought firmly in your mind, savour the moment so that you experience it again – the happy memory will naturally strengthen you because you've surround-ed yourself with good vibes.

Now stand up, take a breath in, let it go and close your eyes. Imagine your body is encircled by a series of golden hoops, forming a moving gyroscope that surrounds you. These are your very own life-enhanc-ing, energy-building rings of confidence and empowerment. Picture this wonderful golden gyroscope spinning all around you. Keep it firmly in your mind's eye. See the golden rings continually turning and moving over and around your body,

> protecting and enclosing you within their gently turning movement.
>
> Tell yourself that this powerful golden gyroscope, your ring of confidence, is here for you in this moment. Feel the power of the moving rings and know they are real for you. When you are ready, say these words: 'I am totally protected in my own force field of energy from this moment on.'

You can do this exercise daily when you get up in the morning and/or after a bath or shower. I create my ring of confidence in a couple of seconds in the morning and then reinstate it whenever the need arises, like when I'm attending a potentially difficult meeting.

You will very quickly notice the positive effect your ring of confidence has on everyone around you, and you will be amazed at how it will attract all that is positive to you, including new friends. However, just as importantly, your ring of confidence will also repel everything that is negative, so it's great to use when you are travelling, walking at night or even just when you're in a crowd. It always works wonders: you just know people sense the power of your energy, but they don't quite know where or what it is!

> I am protecting myself every day, and I'm feeding my energy field and holding anticipation, gratitude and a feeling of abundance for the wishes I've made and am in the process of making.
>
> – **Robert, IT specialist, Birmingham**

26

Thought communication

As you are finding out, your thoughts hold great power and there are many positive ways of using that power. One of the most powerful things you can do with your thoughts is to communicate with other people. Whether it's someone at work, a friend or family member, a partner or a potential lover who you would like to speak to, your projected thought can reach the recipient if you know how to send it.

Think about someone you need to contact right now. When you have them firmly in your mind, stand quietly for a moment, take a breath in and let it go. Now close your eyes, put your hands together in front of you as if in prayer, with your fingers pointing upward above your chest.

In your mind say the person's name three times. Feel the inner glow of your successful 'connection' as you do so – the communication line to them is now open! Then say, '[Person's name], PLEASE contact me now.' Repeat this thought-command three times, then take a breath in, let it go, let your hands part, and smile.

That's all you need do!

The response may happen quickly or not so fast – for some it will be only minutes later that the person gets in touch, for others it may take a few hours – but be assured the recipient will get your message with immediacy. Once received, they will keep hearing and visualising YOU, but it'll be up to them to decide whether to do something about it. Depending on how they feel about you, they may do their utmost to block it – this is their free will.

When I need to speak to someone who knows me, I no longer have to call, email or text them – they always respond to this wonderful message system. I used it just the other day with someone I don't know well. I was meant to be doing a TV interview and hadn't heard anything for a few weeks, so I put the person's name out there and within half an hour there was an email from them confirming the date for the interview.

This way of messaging is a perfect tool to use in our busy world, where everyone is running around distractedly most of the time. While it's great to have the internet and mobile phones, this form of communication allows you to sidestep the new technologies and go straight to whomever it is you need to contact, regardless of where you are.

What you are learning progressively through each of these techniques is how to work your power of thought successfully. Eventually you will come to realise that your potency depends entirely on your own acceptance of the strength of your personal power, your energy level and your true desire to use each of them to achieve results. It is all within your capacity and ability to do so. And once you've got proof of this, it all becomes self-evident and much easier from then on.

On the other hand, if you find you are still caught up in destructive self-talk from your subconscious (which is not surprising, considering how long it's had a hold on you), don't worry. It may take a few weeks of practice before you finally and fully take charge of your Self. Remember, the more you use The Wish techniques and processes, the greater and quicker your empowerment. The main thing is not to give up. This moment is part of your greatest opportunity to create the kind of life in which you can truly blossom and flourish, so don't postpone the chance to enjoy the massive personal fulfilment it will bring.

27

Make it happen

Never a day goes by without us making all sorts of decisions. From the moment we wake up in the morning, decisions have to be made, even if it's just 'Will I have cereal for breakfast, or toast?', 'What do I wear?' or 'Which way should I travel to work?'

Most choices are not choices at all, as we're on automatic. So let me ask you, who is in charge of your decisions? Do you think you are? Think carefully before answering, as you know by now that your subconscious toolbox likes to run very happily on its own without any conscious interference from you. And while that may seem ideal, as there's part of us that would prefer things to carry on as they are, we forget this is what keeps us stuck in the rut of our old patterns, facing the same issues over and over again. It takes conscious, concerted effort to cause a positive shift in your life – so if you want to feel happy and inspired when starting your day, you will need to put in some effort. Why? Because the fight is already on between the 'true you' and the automated system that's running your body.

Let's look at this in a little more depth. When I'm too busy, I find I have difficulty thinking straight and staying focused. For example, when I'm tired after a long day and just want to flop on the couch, then someone will telephone from some other part of the world and expect me to speak to them as if I'm fresh as a daisy! So what do I do? If I want to be in the driver's seat, I have some decisions to make.

Do I take that phone call? The first thing is for me to decide whether I have the reserves to be positive enough before I can even think of answering. Sometimes I know that I have to wait and give myself the chance to 'give thought' to their situation before responding. On other occasions it will be the exact opposite, and these are the times when I get a sensation within me, giving me a positive, energised 'push' to answer the call. This burst of energy comes from my heart/soul connection, and because it knows what is in my best interest to do in that moment, it gives me the go-ahead. If I don't get that energised push then I know the situation isn't urgent and can be resolved at another time. And as I've learned from long experience, you have to feel and be empowered enough to make decisions.

There is, however, no point in having an 'open line' to our soul if we don't listen to it, or if our behaviour doesn't at the same time save and nurture our all – important life energy. Many friends tell me how exhausted they are and how much they need a break, but while they're telling me all this, I notice they're continually texting, updating their Facebook page or answering their mobile phones. All this instant interaction on several levels at once can only be very draining, of that there's no question, but we are also allowing ourselves to be at others' beck and call – they are making the decisions, not us.

Make it happen

You have to remember that you are in charge of you, so it is time to take back control of your life. The following method will assist you greatly in this. It's not just for big decisions – taking charge of the smallest mundane issues in everyday life is every bit as empowering, as it leads naturally on to the bigger ones.

Decision-making has to become a natural part of your daily life if you are ever to increase your self-empowerment. If you feel you have any difficulty with it, start by becoming proactive with the smallest decisions. When you feel like a drink, for example, get up straightaway and make yourself one – do not allow yourself to put it off or become lazy or lax and fall into the same old pattern. 'Immediacy of action' will bring about the necessary change and get you more and more ready to take bigger decisions.

Remember, without decision-making you have no 'boundary', and this effectively means you are continually losing your energy. Basically you're like a sieve, so even though you may exercise and eat well, all that good energy you build up may just keep leaking away. There are many ways you can sense whether or not you're rebuilding your energy or giving it away. One telling scenario is if someone asks you what you would like to do and you simply but honestly answer, 'I don't know' or 'I don't mind'. Not knowing or caring what you want to do only illustrates a lack of empowerment. When you are empowered, and that means feeling good about yourself as well, you would be totally confident to answer the question positively and make a prompt, authoritative decision about what you would really love to do and then feel good about it. And you'll find everyone will respect and appreciate your empowered response.

But don't worry if you feel you're currently indecisive – with practice it all becomes easier for you to be clear about who you are and what you want. Just know that you are worth it. It does take effort, and effort is part of the energy you need, together with enthusiasm, that feeling of excitement for the opportunity that lies before you. You are learning to work with your consciousness with a positive strength of purpose and your own true will.

When it comes to bigger decisions, if you're still

not sure, use the Soul Test from Chapter 19. Always remember to say these words at the beginning of your statement, **'For my highest and greatest good . . .'** The right 'choice' will always give you energy and draw opportunities positively towards you.

As we've discussed, there is an inner knowing within us all, which means you can instinctively sense when you have to do something with immediacy. For example, all of a sudden you think of a close friend or family member who slips into your mind on a thought-wave. You could use logic to stop or ignore it – and then later find out that the person you were thinking of was actually in trouble and needed you. Or alternatively, you can accept the thought-wave for what it is – a message – and call them straightaway. When you follow your intuition you will find it incredibly satisfying, I can assure you, and it's far more likely that both you and they will be staggered at your innate talent to have responded at exactly the right time and to have made the perfect gesture.

As you learn to accept these thought-wave 'prompts', the more regular they will become, continually increasing your power and saving you time and energy. Take note – this is you becoming an intuitively talented and empowered individual!

> **As you learn to accept these thought-wave 'prompts', the more regular they will become, continually increasing your power and saving you time and energy.**

If you are having trouble in making a decision, it is usually due to resistance within you. There are so many decisions we could and should make – but haven't! So pick a decision that you've been avoiding, even a small one, right now. Write down your dilemma on a piece of paper and remember to keep it simple.

Perhaps you have to decide whether or not you want to move house, but don't know what to do. This usually means you either fear change, feel you could be unworthy of anything better, or think you don't have the energy and ability to find a better home at all. How do you change that dynamic? First, you have to implant the belief in yourself. This will come by using a powerful affirmation, which will in turn send out the strong thought-wave to attract what you truly want, in this case the ideal home.

Now find a quiet place. Stand up, take a breath, then let it go and smile. Put your hands, one on top of the other, over your heart and close your eyes. Then say three times, 'I am now moving to the perfect home for me at this time.'

This affirmation not only alters the perceptions you have as to your ability to achieve and move to the ideal home, it will also draw it into your life. It does this by transmitting the positive thought-wave that affirms your ability to be in a home that's right for you, and these vibes can then attract the positive change you are asking for in your life right now. It works, whether it is a new home, relationship, car, holiday or business matter. And every time you succeed, it gives you ever greater power to go on with your decision-making.

IMP

So, having done this exercise, if you feel you're ready for the change, you can then do another Soul Test to determine when this new direction is likely to happen. For example, **'I am now ready for a new car within three months.'**

You will know straightaway from the Soul Test whether you are truly ready to progress and move forward at this time. Trust in your inner knowing. And when you are ready and able to make this leap, there'll be no need to bore your friends by going over the same old doubts, or having sleepless nights about it, because you will know that the power of your destiny is within *you*.

> Now I'm far more decisive and proactive, when I wish for things they do happen. As a result my whole life has shifted . . . I do feel there's a challenge out there and I'm . . . excited about it and can't wait for it, rather than just feeling fed up . . .
>
> – Jenny, human resources manager, London

28

Abundance in all things

When you think about it, everything we've looked at so far is about abundance. It's life-enhancing, empowering, energising, fulfilling, exciting, inspiring, expanding, super-productive, exhilarating, extraordinary – everything that makes life amazing and full of boundless potential. But what does this mean in practical terms? Abundance isn't a word that's used regularly. Maybe that's because it's missing in many lifestyles, almost as if it were well out of most people's reach. Yet when you close your eyes and give thought to abundance, it can quite naturally trigger the most elaborate and delightful imaginings towards everything and anything you feel has been missing in your life. And it's at such moments you need to remind yourself that you are indeed worthy and deserving of genuinely good things, both for your life and in your life.

So let's talk about true abundance. It isn't the latest must-have, most-sought-after consumer item, nor is it having hundreds of friends on the latest internet site or having obscene amounts of money. What I'm talking about here is the *true* wealth of life, the really meaningful things: good health, happiness, laughter, joy, smiles, fond memories, wonderful friends, a loving family and, most importantly, love in everything you do. No doubt you will have your own list of what brings meaning and happiness into your life and what you believe feeds and nurtures your soul. Once you get off that dreadful treadmill the media and the advertisers want to keep you on, your awareness comes alive and life finds a newfound clarity.

There's so many 'I want what they have' attitudes out there, and with them the endless promotion and talk about aspiring to the multimillion-dollar mansion, the yacht and the Ferrari, as if that's the be-all and end-all. But there's very little attention to finding and fulfilling the wealth that really matters – spirituality – which brings about completeness for your highest and greatest good and is the ultimate aspiration for life.

That's why focusing on the heart/soul connection is important as it will elevate all that you bring into your life, positively impacting on you and everyone around you. With this, there is no downside. It is the love inspiration reflected from your heart and generated by your soul, which offers you the highest vibration to give and receive in your life.

You will soon realise that this sort of abundance, once found, is truly 'the magic of being'. As you start to recognise and feel that magic more and more, I assure you that your wildest dreams will begin to flood in, in powerful, life-enforcing and life-enhancing ways. Try treating yourself to finding and achieving one such magical moment each and every day, and you will find an ever-expanding joy quickly building up within you.

We talk a lot about wealth but do we really know what 'wealth' means in the fullest sense? Wealth is commonly understood as meaning that you have large amounts of money, property, assets or other highly valuable possessions, and with them comparable amounts of power, position and control, however temporary. Yet this is such a restricted and limiting view. A person can be wealthy in so many more ways. They may have a wealth of knowledge, for example, like a mentor, teacher or professor, or a wealth of experience and be someone we automatically look up to and ask for help and guidance. Or maybe a wealth of friends, blessed with companions who respect and love them. The potential for vast wealth in any of these areas and more is something you can create and develop for yourself.

Thanks to The Wish I now know that abundance is actually good for my soul and is not something that belongs to other people, or something that I can't have for some kind of religious or other reason. It gives me joy, makes me tingle and makes me know that I actually deserve it and am going to get it.

— Richard, film director, London

Abundance in all things

With your inner knowing comes wisdom and completeness, and your energy field radiates out in all directions. This is true charisma, when your love becomes boundless and you start speaking with genuine feeling, knowledgeably, richly, straight from the heart, without judgement and only with love.

In the end, abundance radiates love. Love knows. It gives you an inner warmth, a sense of feeling good about your Self. Love expands empowerment, thoughtfulness, kindness, generosity, unselfishness, sensitivity and joy. The only restriction we have to abundance is the one we put on ourselves or allow to be put upon us, and this happens when love is absent. In this book you have been taking a good hard look at your life and realising that loving your Self must come first.

True abundance is a joyous and exciting thing. It impacts everyone in the most positive of ways. You automatically access this when you become aware of the phenomenal power you have within you – the power that is held and transmitted by your thoughts.

It therefore stands to reason that if your thoughts

are continually given towards poverty and lack, then you are only going to create the experience of more poverty and lack around you. Whereas if your thoughts are towards wealth and abundance, they will bring more of these to you. What you focus on, you attract. This is not at all about being fixated on wealth, simply a belief that the universe can and will provide all you need to thrive on – and more – when you are ready.

> True abundance is a joyous and exciting thing. It impacts everyone in the most positive of ways.

So have courage to think about your own capacity for abundance, and feel excited at the prospect this opens up for you. Then do the Soul Test to start bringing abundance into your life, using the most stimulating affirmation to benefit the truth of what you can now believe: **'For my highest and greatest good I now have abundance and happiness in my life.'** Say this three times. Keep doing the affirmation once a day for a week, or until you can actually feel the power building within you in every fibre of your body. Your change of attitude will then become your truth, your self – evidence. Then, when you do the Soul Test again, you will naturally find yourself falling forwards. And from then on you will start attracting wealth and money in positive, new and exciting ways.

29

Give to receive

Strange as it may sound, abundance is really not too much to expect when you give thought to the resources already here on our planet which should be 'freely' available to all humanity. By this I mean food, light, energy, water, shelter – the very basics of human life. But centuries have gone by, possibly the whole of this civilisation, where the 'haves' ruled and the 'have-nots' had to accept servitude, living in the most unequal and inharmonious of ways. So despite our recent unparalleled affluence, millions of people continue to starve, while mountains of food are left to rot.

We make a big deal about affluence today, when

really it's poverty in disguise. Affluent people may have a great deal, but sometimes they live as if they have nothing – they know the price of everything but not its value. You might have heard the saying, 'There is nothing meaner than a rich man.' You may even know someone who fits that description. Sadly, there are too many people who will go to the ends of the earth to keep what they've accumulated in terms of money, assets, power and position, and even though some have gained truly vast fortunes, they only use a tiny percentage of their wealth in philanthropic ways. An infamous example of this is Paul Getty, the billionaire who died in 1976, who installed a telephone booth in the entrance hall of his home so guests had to pay if they wanted to make phone calls.

How does the abundance that The Wish offers begin to change all this? How do we turn it around? In your state of completeness, when you're filled with love and able to nurture yourself, you experience continual fulfilment in everything you do. This is truly a sacred place, and when you're in it, it's not hard to be generous or be of service to others. What you then find is that this magically only increases *your own* well-being. You no longer need to live your life through others because you are living in the oneness of life yourself. Your horizons broaden as a result, and the universe is yours, for all you bring to the world. Ultimately this is *unconditional love* – caring and sharing, with empathy and understanding.

The first thing you'll notice is that people you know and meet start treating you differently; some don't react the way they used to, others seem to look at you in a strange way or ask you what you have been doing: you've changed. There will also be remarks on how well you are looking. More importantly, you will find that you attract delightful surprises, like gifts and invitations. People you don't know start talking to you, as they sense you are safe, approachable and positive.

So you truly have to feel good about yourself, know who you are and what your role is in life – and start living all of it to the full. When you reach this place, it is like being the centre of the universe. It gives you the personal authority to ask for whatever you need, because you know who you are, you are sure of yourself and you are not influenced by the spin or manipulative games of others. For now you have what so many crave – the empowerment to do all that you can do – which means you never surrender or give away your true self. Instead, you can stay in what I call 'observer' mode, without attachment or judgement, and with a healthy boundary around your life force, a golden line between you and others. Your energy is protected, nurtured and used wisely, while sharing and giving out boundless love and generosity of spirit to everyone and everything around you.

To help you step into the full abundance of giving and receiving, let's take a closer look at what may still be holding you back. When we talk about abundance, we're not talking about greed, because greed is never for your highest good – it can only ever bring emptiness and unhappiness. Greed is a desire that goes awry when it is uncontrolled through your will – leading it to become one of the most negative driving forces in life. Greed is active; it creates a vacuum within you that forever requires filling, an incessant desire to have more and still more.

The Wish

I believe greed is perfectly described as an intense human desire for all that is material and physical. So therein lies power, money, gold, titles, possessions and awards, and with them conceit, arrogance, ego and selfishness. The intensity of desire can only turn everything into a 'must-have' – whether that's the biggest yacht in the marina, the best house in the street, the flashiest car, the largest corner office, the best table in the restaurant, the swankiest party.

Henry Kissinger was once quoted as saying, 'Power is the greatest aphrodisiac.' At first this may sound intriguing and even appealing but there's very little in it to feed your soul, let alone say anything about happiness and well-being, or having the genuine love and respect of those around you, or the sheer joy of getting out of bed in the morning and feeling in tune with the world, or being alive and connected to the best things in life as a whole.

Another face of greed is one of entitlement, of controlling and demanding in a different way, driven to acquire due to an apparent lack of status or position. Here, you'll find an individual's attitude expressing 'I'm owed' or 'I take', instead of the simple 'I want'. These needy individuals often fall victim to 'hyper-moods'. They may be so desperate in their desires that they become aggressive and violent or fall into addictive behaviour patterns. This can happen when people want to dull their feelings of unhappiness. They fill the void with chocolate, shopping or, worse, alcohol or drugs, looking for pleasure and happiness, however short-lived. Then, if they're not in control of their subconscious, it only nags at them to repeat the sensation a little later. And the more the void inside them is fed, the greater the hunger.

Do take time to observe these types of people. You can easily catch them on TV any night of the week, whether in the political, entertainment or sporting realms. The underlying ego becomes easy to spot once you see through the glamour and the spin they hide behind – life is all about them after all. Inevitably their lives will spin out of control, often spectacularly – be it through sex, drugs or corruption – because they hadn't the benefit of the rock-solid foundation the heart/soul connection brings.

The irony is that these needy people are driven to extremes by an overwhelming sense of lack. They may seem to have everything, but they have never experienced true abundance. When these people are ready to acknowledge and recognise their behaviour pattern, they are well on the way to altering their automatic response patterns.

The Wish process helps you to recognise and clear any associations and connections you may have of 'lack', for this is the void that becomes the vacuum. 'Lack of knowing', for example, brings about fear and is mentally and physically disabling, disarming and self-destructive. Similarly when you 'lack a sense of Self', where you've lost or forgotten the importance of love of self: until you rediscover that love inside, you will be unable to feel complete, and this shows up in envy and jealousy. Then there's 'lack of self-fulfilment'. This can easily spill out into selfishness and become a terrible negative: 'me, me, me'. For example, when an ageing relative expects you to care for them, regardless of any plans you might have.

When we begin to think in terms of 'I have no

money' that lack can only increase. Remember, if your thoughts are continually about how poor you are, or how close you are to poverty, or how you are experiencing any great lack of something, then you are only creating and attracting the experience of still more poverty and lack towards you. So every time you fall into a sense of 'lack', remember this is but a step away from abundance and that delicious feeling of completeness we all crave.

Love comes first and foremost in everything, and this must include loving yourself enough to know your identity and your true role in life. No 'this will do', no second-best, no half measures. Once you stand in the strength of who you are and what you are worth, there is nothing you cannot achieve. As you delve deeper into the principle of true abundance, you will begin to see how giving is just as important as receiving. Ultimately, whatever you do in life, the motto 'Giving for receiving' is the gem I ask you to remember the most.

I was in the supermarket one day and queuing at the checkout (as always, it seems!), when a very polite elderly lady with vision problems asked me if I could please check her purse and tell her if she had enough money to pay for the items she had in her basket. I noticed that her meagre items were all essentials for everyday living, yet she didn't have enough money. Discreetly I put my hand into my wallet and slipped a note into her purse, then told her she had absolutely the right money! She was so relieved, telling me she didn't get her pension for another couple of days and was so worried about what she had left. Later that day I stopped off at a shop and, in a rush, grabbed what I needed, paid and went home. The next morning I realised I had an extra note in my wallet – how did it get there? I could only think that the second shop had given it to me in error. So what comes around goes around. Life goes full circle – you give in one direction and it comes back in another.

As you delve deeper into the principle of true abundance, you will begin to see how giving is just as important as receiving.

It is when we only expect and then take it (whatever 'it' is, large or small, cheap or expensive) with no thought to give or give back, that we have bought the one-way ticket into the endless vacuum of greed.

It's also important to remember that when you give in order to 'rescue' someone, you in turn become a 'victim' of the person you have rescued. As hard as it may seem, sympathising with those who are locked into victim-consciousness will only support their victim-hood – and tie you to them. Victim-consciousness is a mindset, pure and simple, where the victim is expecting someone to come and save them.

'Giving' is part of gratitude – and your gratitude for being here at this time starts the flow of abundance fulfilling your life. You have surely noticed that every time you give in any way you get a buzz of energy that makes you feel alive, fresh and greatly energised. Your abundance naturally spills out to benefit others: one day it may be the donation of some spare change to a street appeal, or giving clothes you no longer wear to the local charity shop, or it may be a modest donation to help the relief effort after an international disaster. Perhaps you may even prefer to take independent action yourself and assist people or animals you know could benefit from a helping hand. This is the shape and taste of true abundance – happiness glows within you, radiating far beyond, with wonderful feelings of joy.

All this is beyond riches and is true, unconditional love. When you're living with a heart/soul connection and plugged into what's for your highest good, you begin to understand the power of one – the complete soul-being radiating within you. And then you become naturally intuitive and empathetic towards others, humanity and the world as a whole – you are fully and completely a worthy, living and loving part of the universe.

30

Your perfect health and weight

We've already talked about good health being part of an abundant life. Here, I'll give you an easy but effective exercise to speed you on your way. It's also brilliant for arriving at your perfect weight, whether you want to put on weight or lose it. You can also use it for boosting and strengthening your immune system.

I had put on two stone (13 kg) in two years and was having trouble shifting the weight. After completing The Wish course I made a wish that I wanted to lose the weight through a diet and exercise program that I would be able to maintain . . . I have integrated this into my lifestyle and have lost one and a half stone

(9 kg) in four months with little effort – eating food I
love and enjoying exercise whenever I feel like it.

– Pauline, record producer, New York

Very few people are always happy with their weight,
but before we start, it's crucial to be realistic – by that
I mean seeking your healthy weight. It's important to
mention this because when it comes to weight I've
found the majority of people have a false perception
of what their true weight should be, often seeking
their ideal 'dream look' based more on a role model
on TV or in a magazine than what suits their own body
shape and size. With this exercise, though, you can
check out the weight you think you should be and
then find out whether you're right. This is because the
Soul Test will only tell you the truth of what your
perfect weight is – no ifs and buts about it! And that
means the weight that benefits your physical body,
given optimum health.

Begin by writing down what you think your perfect
weight should be. And please try to be in the right

ball-park to start with, otherwise the Soul Test will only have you falling backwards while you keep getting it wrong! Now, stand up and do the Soul Test using these words: 'My perfect weight is [whatever you think is realistically your perfect weight].' Repeat the words three times.

Did you fall forwards? If yes, then you know the perfect body weight for you.

If you didn't move at all, try it again. Some of us have bodies that stay healthier when they fluctuate between two weights, as mine does. So I say, for example, 'My perfect weight is 54 to 55 kilograms.'

If you fall backwards, then you have to keep trying until you get the true weight for you.

When you know your perfect weight, find somewhere quiet (no phones!) with a comfortable chair. Sit down and tell yourself to relax. Take a breath in, and let it go; do this three times.

Visualise a large cinema screen in front of you; give it a bright blue surround or frame. Then see yourself on the screen. If you have difficulty with visualising this, then talk yourself through it

217

instead and tell yourself you are on the screen in front of you.

Now see yourself, on that screen, full of zest for life and moving around – walking, jogging, running as though you were doing a fitness regime. See yourself looking amazing and fantastic. Know that this is you, and see and feel how great you look. Take a breath in and let it go. Smile. Then close down the screen.

Now stand up and do the Soul Test again, using these words: 'My body is now maintaining its perfect health and weight at [whatever weight you now know you can be].' Repeat the words three times.

Did you fall forwards? If you did, then great! You have acknowledged your perfect look and weight for living. Your body has taken on the command and will now start to adjust, naturally reprogramming itself to bring about the perfect altered state.

If you didn't move, or you fell backwards, then do the Soul Test twice a day until your body accepts the commands and falls forward. It may take a couple of days for it to fully sink in, but do not give up – you are in charge and this really works. Once done, your body will slowly and safely readjust to find your health, if necessary gaining or shedding the weight it needs to.

I found my 'perfect weight' allowed me to shift it up and down by a kilo or so, giving me the wonderful potential to enjoy any food I wished for at least some of the time without worrying that I was going over the top: I knew I could very quickly shed it by using this method when I needed to later on, and on average I do have to give my body a reminder once a year to stay in check. It is so simple and extremely empowering.

31

Check out your gratitude

We have come to the ideal moment to consider gratitude. This is a thought process that, once started, links you to a feeling of excitement and triggers a positive response. As soon as you feel good about yourself, you are thankful. You feel loved and it excites you, knowing that your life has endless opportunities for you, and with an overwhelming surge of love inside that infiltrates everything. It is at this moment you have gratitude for your very being, for your life and all the potential it has to offer – you become optimistic about everything.

When you receive a gift, win a prize or are congratulated for your work, these are moments when your gratitude can shine – you know it is great to be alive. You feel loved, wanted and worthy. What you put out there comes back a hundredfold.

> **When you receive a gift, win a prize or are congratulated for your work, these are moments when your gratitude can shine.**

When you don't have that respect, or any appreciation for the events you have managed up to this moment in your life, it can only reduce and greatly undermine your potential for gratitude. And without gratitude for living you will always continue to miss out on fulfilment and contentment in your life.

We have all met people who are continually critical of others – at the office, in a shop, ahead of you in a long post office queue, at the bus stop, or on the train. These people are only deflecting their own 'lack' and become increasingly negative (sometimes to the point of aggression), completely wasting valuable energy. It's the same for jealous people who have the attitude that 'I should be getting that' or 'That should have been me'. They are all caught up in their own self-absorption. Until they look inside themselves and start building themselves up from within, learning how to love themselves and realising they alone hold the key to self-empowerment and true fulfilment, gratitude and generosity of spirit will always evade them.

There is an old man with a little shop in India who I have got to know well over the years. He sells the most wonderful trinkets, jewellery and crystals, and I take many customers to him. I suggested he should consider giving his customers a small gift with each sale; I explained that this was 'giving for receiving' and that his generosity of spirit would then bring him much more business. He decided to follow my suggestion and he gives each of his customers the gift of a gem when they purchase something from him. The gift might not be of great value in terms of money, but it is of great value to the customers – and him, too – for it is done with gratitude.

Check out your gratitude

Here is a quick way to check your gratitude:

Give a score for each of the following statements from 1 to 7, with 7 = strongly agree and 1 = strongly disagree.

7 A. I have so much in life to be thankful for.

7 B. If I listed all I'm grateful for it would be a long list.

7 C. I am grateful to a wide variety of people.

7 D. As I grow older I find I am more able to appreciate other people, events and situations.

Add together your scores for A to D: Total ___ 28

For the following two statements, again give a score from 1 to 7; this time 7 = strongly disagree and 1 = strongly agree.

1 E. When I view the world I see little to be grateful for.

1 F. A lot of time goes by before I feel grateful to anyone or anything.

The Wish

Add together your scores for E to F: Total _____ 2

YOUR TOTAL SCORE: Add the total scores for A–D
and E–F: _____ 30

14 or less: You are on the bottom rung for gratitude
– it is time to feel love and good grace.
15–28: You are in the lower half of the gratitude
scale, and not yet a 'giver'. Start reminding yourself
daily to create generosity of spirit, of giving for
receiving.
29–36: You have love within you and, with gratitude,
are acknowledging the existence of other people
living on our planet.
37–42: You have learned much from experience, you
journey with love in your heart and soul. You
resonate on a high frequency in the top spiritual
echelon of our world.

If your score is low, it's easy to build up an inner sense
of gratitude, where you truly feel good to be alive and
have a natural connection to people around you. Many

people make the terrible mistake of thinking they are separate from others and not a part of all creation.

To increase your gratitude, first give thought to the number of situations that have arisen in the past when someone has been 'giving' towards you. It could be a colleague simply sharing their umbrella or offering you a lift in their car, or maybe someone cooking you a meal, buying you a surprise theatre ticket or offering to help you move house. These are all moments when gratitude can be joyfully expressed, so from this moment on make an effort to be grateful for the many everyday kindnesses shown and given to you, and begin making your own thoughtful gestures – those that come from your heart – in return; the inner joy you receive will increase with each and every act.

32

Enlighten your thought

As I think it, so shall it be . . .

'Thought' is the ultimate means for true empowerment. It literally offers you everything from here to eternity. When recognised and fully worked, it has the highest potential for all of us. Thought can be expanded to give you greater vision, when transmitted it is enabling, and when received it is assuring. As you boost your energy or excitement about something you want to create, you have the potential to manifest an outcome way beyond all your expectations. Once mastered, the power of your unleashed thought is the most exciting knowledge I can share with you to benefit your life from now on.

Enlighten your thought

We've all heard it said that humans use only 10 per cent of their brains. In my opinion the greatest resource still lying dormant and waiting to be fired up and made fully operational is 'conscious directed thought'. And all it needs to ignite that spark is for you to realise that with the help of your own will you have the capability to dramatically increase its usage.

> **The power of your unleashed thought is the most exciting knowledge I can share with you to benefit your life from now on.**

Every strong thought emits its own waveform. This waveform then becomes a telepathic link between you and the rest of life and transmits signals outside the human body.

As a twin, my telepathic link has never dulled. In my work of mediumship, receiving information from those I call 'spirit people', I rely on their ability to send me telepathic thought-waves so that I pass on what can often be extremely complex messages or information to the recipient, sometimes using words or in a language completely unknown to me.

In a directed thought (and by that I mean one that holds some significance or meaning to you, as opposed to a random, fleeting thought) the waveform actually creates shape and colour. This can be picked up and seen in your aura, the energy field around your head. So when it is an angry thought, the waveform thrown out has streaks of red that can be felt or at least sensed by the recipient (hence the old expression 'seeing red'). Other negative thoughts will be tinged with dark grey and brown shadows.

When you direct your focus on the thought and give it shape, colour and movement, it maintains its dynamics and is literally brought to life. These aspects give your thought its real power, strength and depth. The next step is to create enough positivity within yourself to begin manifesting that thought. This is because thought needs energy to bring it to life. Thought, and the vast power it can generate and contain, goes way beyond the boundaries of the mind and physical body – it transcends time and distance.

Now we come to the most exciting step to benefit and assist you when you start actually making your wish. We begin by practising how to focus your thought.

Sit comfortably, close your eyes, take a breath in and let it go. Repeat two more times. Relax! Fill your mind with a very pleasurable memory, one that gives you a feeling of happiness and excitement – it could be that very first, hesitant kiss, or that life-changing feeling when you realised you had fallen in love, or when you were given a wonderful surprise gift, enjoyed a great celebration or finally achieved a long-cherished ambition.

Once you have that special memory clearly in your mind, concentrate and focus all of your thought on reliving that moment – what you see, hear and feel with that wonderful memory. Start to become part of it again, in every way you can, moment by moment, using every sense, every emotion you have available to you. Rekindle the feelings of joy, pleasure, excitement, delight, happiness that it gave you. Relive every one of the feelings that you felt before, enjoy it as it happens all over again. Feel deep within you that growing pleasure, that thrill and sensuality of really being a part of it once more.

This is the power of 'focusing your thought', consciously directing your thought, where you become wholly part of the experience. Notice again how you're harnessing the shape, colour and movement of this memory to bring it to life.

DO NOT give in to any self-doubt.

Remember the importance of all your learning: **YOU** are going to make **YOUR** wish for what **YOU** *really* want, completely and wholeheartedly believing in the strength of your thought power to create it.

It is vital that you get this right, so think of another example to help you see – and feel – exactly what I mean. Take a few more moments and give thought to another past, happy and truly memorable experience that you can conjure and experience as if it happened only yesterday. Take yourself back to that moment and relive it. Don't forget to see it, hear it, and really feel the sensations you then had within you.

The more focused your thought and the greater the intensity of your desire, the greater the opportunity you will find and have for creating endless and boundless opportunities in your life from now on. Remember, you can wish for whatever you really want to make manifest, whether it's big or small.

I'm using The Wish for both major and minor things in my life. Shortly after doing The Wish I used it for small things like moving through traffic in the city and finding parking spaces – I found it really made a difference, as one can become very wound up in a traffic situation and when we used the tools from the course, it all moved so much better and more smoothly . . . I also use The Wish for the big things in my life, and two of them have already come through for me – the perfect home and the school of choice for my children.

– **Robert, IT specialist, Birmingham**

The Wish

Before you actually create your wish, let's go back through the process we have completed so far together:

You know yourself: you know your true identity and purpose in life.

You are in control and understand your past fears.

You hold a deep connection between your heart and your Soul: you are one.

You have acknowledged the importance of decision-making.

Your self-worth is at an all-time high.

You know how to focus your intention.

Congratulate yourself for having achieved so much to reach this exciting moment. But if for any reason you still do not feel you are ready, go back to repeat any area where you are uncertain. This will give you that extra boost and confidence to proceed.

33

Create your wish

Now you are ready for lift-off, for the final step on the path to making your wish and many more come true. Take a deep breath – here goes!

First, just before I am going to make a powerful wish, I allow myself time to sit and give thought to exactly what I'm going to wish for and how I see it taking place in my life, what it feels like when it's here 'now'. This is vitally important – there is no question it will come into being; it is more the conscious recognition of this wish coming true and being part of my life from this moment on, and my gratitude and excitement for it as it assists my fulfilment.

Having done this I am absolutely ready to create, in the knowledge that I love everything it represents for me from this moment on. So take a moment to contemplate the good that can flow from your wish.

See it, feel it, know it . . .

Remember your wish is your own creation, not mine or anyone else's. Everything that takes place from now on is going to be, and can only be, based on YOUR positive thought-intention. Remember also that it is exactly as if you are already living your wish in reality, in the flesh, and so it is already part of your life right now.

Now feel the excitement growing as it wells up inside you. Surrender to it. Really give in to feeling that your wish is about to come true. Feel the sensation that starts with that inner warmth inside; enjoy it as it continues to build, glowing and resonating upwards and outwards, roused with anticipation and fired with a sudden inner knowing that you're fully in the zone, right in the 'now'. You are ready. You're right on the edge of 'making it happen' with your wish.

Create your wish

Hold this feeling right here! Before you begin
finally making your wish, the simple rules to remember are:

Decide on one thing: something you truly want in
   your life.
Do not specify how your wish is to come about, only
   that 'it is'.
Feel calm, prepared and organised.
Sit, relax and sense a growing excitement towards
   what you are about to create.
Take a few breaths in and out and close your eyes.

When you are ready, say these words in your mind:
'This is my greatest opportunity to create.' Then,
using your strongest thought-commands to create
exactly what you wish, give it depth and make it a
'sense-surround' film that you're taking part in, you
are in the film. Give it detail, movement and action
by giving your wish shape, colour and movement.
Make sure you are deep within it, playing your part,
involved in the very centre of your own creation.

The Wish

Now focus every atom, all of your thought-intention, on your wish. Create it right now. Your wish is the film taking place at this moment all around you, in front of you, behind you. You are in this film and really experiencing it, feeling it, enjoying it, smelling it, tasting it. Know you are actually taking part and sense the enjoyment and power of your wish happening, pulsating through you as it does so.

See your wish vividly through the *command of your mind*. It is alive with shape, colour and movement, a richly visual, tactile, sensual, physical, emotional experience. Talk yourself through your wish and feel the increasing excitement and joy it has for you as the anticipation builds up. You are in the film, you *are* the film as it is taking place.

And at the precise moment when you are feeling and experiencing the peak of all these thoughts, these sensations, these actions, take the whole of that vast well of emotion and gather it into a large golden-yellow balloon. Then place your special balloon at head height right in front of you. It now contains and holds every atom and fibre of your wish experience.

Create your wish

When your balloon is right in front of you, see a large round golden doorway opening up ahead of you. It is an opening, a doorway into another, parallel dimension. Now, using all the power of your intention, push your golden-yellow balloon with your wish inside it through that opening, saying these words: 'I NOW RELEASE MY WISH.'

Then command the doorway to close. See the door close . . . and know your wish has now been released into the endless resources of the universe. Take a deep breath and smile – 'YES'.

Feels good, doesn't it? You have just released your wish. There is no attachment to it now. It can safely take its journey travelling through the parallel dimension. And as it does so, the energy that you have created will be expanding and ever-increasing, allowing endless and boundless opportunities to enter your life. Your wish is on its journey and will arrive in this physical dimension when it is the perfect time for it to manifest.

From now on, hold and maintain a feeling of

anticipation through this 'knowing' that *you* have created *your* wish. Feel the strength and depth of the emotion that welled up inside you. Keep this strength and knowing, and let it increase in this moment, and from now on. Enjoy the experience with gratitude and love.

Congratulations on creating your very own wish – for you and you alone – in the 'now'!

Yet, is there more? Oh yes, so much more. From now on, you can create any wish you want in your life in a moment. It doesn't matter if the wishes are small, medium or large, as you now have the golden key of knowledge about how to create them for yourself. It is an understanding of the divine creation of your being in existence, working through your heart and soul.

In a nutshell, it's a pure sense of love.

For me [the power of The Wish] has mainly been the realisation that you can, with focused creative thought, control what is happening in your life and take it in a very positive direction, and see in a very short space of time the effect it has on people – the

Create your wish

effect that we have on people to make a
change . . . In very small subtle ways you can make
such a difference.

– Pauline, record producer, New York

34

The ultimate arrival

Now you have learned the secrets of The Wish, you hold in your keeping some of the most powerful tools you will ever encounter. So there's no need to miss any more opportunities that come your way. Your mission now is to go beyond the ordinary mundane matters of everyday life. Your ultimate aim must be to reach for the highest possible goals in life, to be the very best you can be, according to the wisdom and insight you gain from your heart/soul connection. This is achievable for each and every one of you, once you realise you are here on your chosen spiritual journey – a journey meant for you to nourish yourself, body and spirit. When you take this path you recognise your uniqueness and become complete in every aspect of your life.

> **Your ultimate aim must be to reach for the highest possible goals in life, to be the very best you can, according to the wisdom and insight you gain from your heart/soul connection.**

The true quest is in finding completeness *within* you. There are two ways that your soul and the power of thought can affect your life from here on. The first is to be very careful what you wish for – yes, that old but very true adage. That's why it's so important to truly sense what it's like to live your wish before you create it – that way you really know what it'll feel like to live your wish and be clear that it's genuinely going to enhance your life.

The second is, as you now know, the importance of living life with your own soul's truth. So from now on spend a moment or two considering whether you are or should ever be surrendering your own power to anyone else. After all, you have worked hard to build up your vibrant, energetic self. You now know *who* you are, what your passions and life purpose are, and where you need to head to fulfil your life's destiny. So why give it all away to somebody else? There will always be part of you that, in a weak moment, may be tempted to let someone take over the reins, but as you now know, that's not what makes dreams and wishes come true. It is *you* who makes the decisions now, as a self-responsible being. It is *you* who can shift your life whatever the circumstances you are in. And, if you need additional resources, the universe is part of you and will help draw them to you. So make a plan and do it. No 'what ifs', 'buts' or 'maybes'. You are worth it. Always endeavour to be your own person, and bring about a whole new way of living for yourself in the now. Your destination is now within reach. I call it the 'ultimate arrival'. It comes about by actually creating and turning the wish, or wishes, you dreamed of into reality.

Having released your wish, it is now time to

embrace the immediacy of opportunities, happenings and encounters that will start appearing in your life in the most exciting and amazing ways. It is also a time when signposts spring up – usually when they are least expected – and quite naturally inspire us to look that little bit further or harder in order to seek out more knowledge. And now those fears are recognised and understood, there is so much more to gain from taking a leap forward to defeat them forever, in turn benefiting your Self and progressing your own life dramatically.

Now you have successfully expanded your awareness, nothing will seem to stay the same in your life. Your perception has transcended the old mindset and long overtaken that old belief system. Your challenge now is to live life to the full using the courage it gives you, and to make the very most of the empowerment that you have at your fingertips. You have both the power and the know-how, so that with just a few moments' careful reflection you can use your thoughts to send out the amazing waveforms that will attract what you wish for. All that then remains is how you decide to follow your newly laid path of attraction.

> Your challenge now is to live life to the full using the courage it gives you, and to make the very most of the empowerment that you have at your fingertips.

My advice would be to start simply. Learn to gauge your newfound power little by little. Perhaps be a little wary, given you have made a very major leap forward and now hold significant abilities beyond all previous imaginings. Your empowerment through the use of focused thought can literally 'make it happen' whenever you want. And by knowing your true role you can bring about the complete fulfilment you seek. All the chess pieces will start to move into the right positions as you create your ideal life from now on, benefiting every part of you and reflecting well on others.

Never forget this is possible because of the

immense love and gratitude you have for the life you create. Love creates more love. As long as your wish is inspired by your heart/soul connection and not by need, once gained and held you can be sure that your fulfilment will continue to resonate all around you in all areas of your life, attracting all that is positive and beneficial while eliminating all negative energies.

Now you have at last taken that massive leap of trust in yourself by trying out The Wish principles, you can afford to relax a little and ask yourself just what it was that stopped you doing what you wished for before. For some of you, no doubt it would be because you didn't feel you had the power or ability; while others were simply searching for the know-how to work your magic. Perhaps your parents and their parents before them never had the opportunity to find and enjoy such exceptional personal power. Yet it has been lying dormant in us all along, just waiting to be triggered into action.

Think about the enormity of this. You are the lucky one, because you have been given the keys. You have what so many of those who have come before you ached for. So give gratitude for the leaps and bounds you have made, and for the time you live in. Think about the gifts of modern technology. Over the past 60 years or so it has offered us ever more incredible opportunities to spend time on ourselves, easier and easier ways of connecting with more and more people, the chance to learn so many new skills, ways to relax or entertain, and to enjoy so many other benefits.

This period is perhaps the first time in the history of our civilisation that we have the opportunity, the freedom of choice, to seek out and find any information we choose. This enables us to expand our horizons on many levels, including the quest towards greater spiritual knowledge. This, in turn, leads us to exciting new horizons that transcend the current, limiting beliefs. We have broadened communication with each other to a level never before realised. It is such a progressive step that I feel without a shadow of a doubt we are – in this sense at least – living in a new 'golden era'. Everything is out there when we are ready to assimilate the learning. Now boundless possibilities are readily available to us.

So, as you begin living your manifested wishes, how can you then work your growing magic towards assisting others to find their awareness to achieve their own dreams or goals? And in turn, how can they then, quite naturally, start spreading their magic from person to person, friend to friend, multiplying exponentially around the globe, to benefit people from all walks of life at whatever stage they are at right now? Just think of the range of possibilities those 'wishes' could cover: abundance of pure drinking water, a plot of land to grow food, a home people can call their own, a safe environment to live in, like-minded friendships, the chance for an education. The list of wonderful, life-changing opportunities is limitless.

So many of these things are taken for granted in the West because we have so much. What we begin to wake up to is how much power we have to transform the lives of others. With your assistance we can share the tremendous potential for happy, fulfilled, dignified lives with a far greater proportion of humanity by using the power of our – and their – manifested wishes to enlighten and empower those in terrible need. Then others, too, can find and believe in themselves, realise their nascent abilities and begin working for the highest and greatest good of all.

> **What we begin to wake up to is how much power we have to transform the lives of others.**

The wonderful thing is you can become an active participant in this exhilarating process without even leaving your home. You can simply spend a few moments focusing your attention on 'intention' towards the 'highest and greatest good of all' and inviting those 'like-minded' friends you know to join you when doing so. As they spread the word, sooner or later everyone will want to join in.

There are some fun aspects to this as well. Why not enjoy a positively energised afternoon or evening by getting together with friends of like mind to make a wish each for yourselves, and for the benefit of the world, its protection and enlightenment with love? People just love the idea of 'sharing a wish' in a group. Select one idea to focus on and wish for. Whether it's once a week or once a month doesn't matter, it's the collective energy you can generate together that's so powerful. Of course, someone will have to take everyone else through the process. Harness your combined concentrated thought, put it out there together with everything you've got, and when the wish moment comes you will create a vast waveform that will manifest with tremendous immediacy. It really is that powerful.

When, for example, three of you do this together – there's that wonderful power of three again – the energy build-up has a huge, ever-expanding effect as you blend your consciousness together. From experience I know the group power of three, five, seven, ten (or even more) holds an extreme resonance in frequency that is truly amazing and has an effect readily felt by everyone. This can be very valuable when sending love and healing to someone or when creating a very positive thought on a specific issue you all care about. I did this recently in London with a whole group of friends. We focused on some of the huge issues facing our planet at present. It was a fun gathering, the energy was forever increasing because we loved being together. And when it came time to create our wish for the world, it was an unbelievably powerful moment and celebration.

The Wish is a great gift for our children as well. They are the future. Unlike us they have an innocent open curiosity towards life, a lot of magic that we have to work hard to recapture, so The Wish principles are almost second nature to them. Children simply pick up the idea of how to 'create' in seconds, in mere moments, and show true delight when their wish comes true. To them, all things are still wonderfully and amazingly possible, so it's important to keep this exquisite faculty alive. A great bonus for them is that they can then move with less baggage towards adult life.

The ultimate arrival

The Wish is a great gift for our children as well. They are the future.

As you have found – and now will continue to experience – you can recover that childlike delight in 'creation' and use it as an adult in everyday life. The ability to focus your thought you now have can blend with the focused thoughts of other like-minded people and become capable of very powerful manifestation, not only in your life but in the lives of all those around you.

Congratulations! You have now made that conscious shift you longed for when you picked up this book and a switch has triggered in your head, making possible what was previously impossible. Your heightened awareness now empowers your whole being. Embrace what life now offers you with joy and gratitude. And stay pro-active, focused and involved in your wish for the future from this moment on. Enjoy the magic of life and all it now brings you.

'I was looking for something further in my life,

251

so when I heard about The Wish it seemed like a natural progression,' explains Chris, a marketing executive in London. 'I made it my wish to marry the girl of my dreams.' Five months later Andrew and I were delighted to attend their most amazing wedding.

35

My wish for life

*It is not the deed, but the thought
behind the deed . . .*

When I successfully completed the 'Make It Happen
with The Wish' coursework, I sat quietly for a
moment and then wrote out my own mission statement for this lifetime. Taking care with my use of
words, something I always try to do, I stated, *'Through
my own self-awareness and spirituality, to act as a
sharer and mentor to assist others who seek to know
on their path to enlightenment.'*

As I have now become fully aware of my role in
this life so too can you, by taking that cosmic leap to a

truly great level of conscious creative imagination. After all you've learned perhaps you will also be inspired to hold a bigger vision. By being well practised in The Wish approach to life, I live in the joy and abundance of my thought creations. What I've discovered is how synchronicities abound. Now even my momentary thoughts work at an alarming speed, to the extent that when I sit for even a moment and focus a thought on someone or something, there is an occurrence very soon after.

For these reasons, I have learned to be exceedingly careful with my thoughts and my time, let alone the things I wish for! Simply losing myself in research work is not enough, for as soon as I start questioning details and facts about what I'm researching, powerful thought forms are emitted and within the very same week I end up meeting the particular person involved in that subject or finding whatever material I need. I am constantly amazed by how much my soul supports my life in this way, and every time am in awe of it as a child would be.

To me, all of life is a holiday. I don't say this lightly

or flippantly, but to express the joy and ease I now experience. I am self-fulfilled and self-motivated in the way I speak my truth with a resounding enthusiasm, and my energy increases exponentially as a result. I'm constantly humbled by the feedback I get from my teaching, how inspired people are, how profoundly their lives change, because this is my profoundest wish. Having made my heart/soul connection I know this is what I'm meant to be here for. It's a huge privilege to do my life's work, the work that I love, with all my heart and soul, and that is my gift to you.

As you now know, The Wish is the big picture of existence. It's the magical gem of evidence required for knowing, unleashing your power positively to make it happen in your life in the now. It is surely the most exciting adventure ever created by thought creation. Since starting to teach The Wish course I have been overwhelmed with the results and The Wish has assisted me in knowing my purpose, knowing my role, because I could think of it in a broader context than just my daily life or my daily work. Sean, a finance director based in Tokyo, told me, 'It gave me a perspective that really stretches across my family, across all people on the planet and maybe even across generations to come. It has made a dramatic change in me and my perception in life, and that comes from knowing who I am and my place in the universe.'

When you have been exposed to what the universe offers you, you realise how limiting our everyday belief systems and education are. With The Wish, however, you get the opportunity to expand your mind to the greatest extent possible, to view all that is out there. This, in turn, gives you the opportunity to access and open up your full potential consciousness, to come spiritually alive and transcend all limitations, thereby discovering new horizons and new dimensions to life, way beyond the restrictions of the normal belief system you have been educated in and equipped with.

So let's drop all the clutter and travel light! It is my wish with this book to give everyone the greatest opportunity to 'wake up' by means of a call that acts as a common spiritual awakening which can then expand globally. Sometimes we need to be reminded that there is an immense power available, right here under our noses so to speak, just ready and waiting for us to realise and ignite. And it has always been here, we only have to seek it out and learn how to use it, and then we can reap all the benefits it offers and allows.

With The Wish you get the experience and self-knowledge to recognise your will as the very greatest power you can work with. So, smiling as I complete The Wish process, let me give you a gentle reminder not to lose your sense of humour, for it is that sense of laughter that warms the heart and resonates all around, crossing all faiths, creeds, colours and persuasions, boosts your body's health and immune system and – most importantly – brings joy to life. Never forget you have at your disposal a wise soul energy that knows and can affect all you wish for; it connects you directly to the Source of the Universe itself, and within it the Source of Knowledge and Wisdom that can be called upon at any time, any day you choose. It is limitless.

Doing what you are truly meant to be doing, being

who you truly are meant to be, makes life the greatest opportunity for every second it lasts. Nothing is wasted and everything encountered has been a learning when freedom of choice and all that you wish for are truly your own.

If you've loved *The Wish*,
why not share the magic and let
your friends know.

www.thewish.com.au